ACTS 20

FIERCE WOLVES ARE COMING;
GUARD THE FLOCK

A Study of Paul's Final Charge
to the Ephesian Elders

Alexander Strauch

Other books by Alexander Strauch include:

Biblical Eldership:
An Urgent Call to Restore Biblical Church Leadership

The Study Guide to Biblical Eldership:
Twelve Lessons for Mentoring Men for Eldership

Meetings That Work

The Hospitality Commands

Agape Leadership:
Lessons in Spiritual Leadership from the Life of
R. C. Chapman (Coauthored with Robert L. Peterson)

Men and Women: Equal Yet Different

A Christian Leader's Guide to Leading With Love

Love or Die:
Christ's Wake-Up Call to the Church, Revelation 2:4

If You Bite and Devour One Another:
Biblical Principles for Handling Conflict

Paul's Vision for the Deacons:
Assisting the Elders with the Care of God's Church

The 15 Descriptions of Love:
Applied to All Christian Leaders & Teachers

Acts 20

FIERCE WOLVES ARE COMING
— GUARD THE FLOCK —

A STUDY OF PAUL'S FINAL CHARGE
TO THE EPHESIAN ELDERS

Lewis & Roth Publishers

Acts 20: Fierce Wolves are Coming; Guard the Flock
ISBN-10: 0936083751
ISBN-13: 9780936083759
Copyright © 2021 by Alexander Strauch. All rights reserved.

Cover design & typesetting: Bryana Mansfield

Printed in the United States of America
Second Printing 2021

Library of Congress Control Number: 2020939280

To receive a free catalog of books published by Lewis and Roth
Publishers, please call toll free 800-477-3239 or visit our website
www.LewisandRoth.com. If you are calling from outside the United States,
please call 719-494-1800.

Lewis and Roth Publishers
307 Delaware Drive
Colorado Springs, Colorado 80909

CONTENTS

ABBREVIATIONS

1. Old Testament

Gen.	Genesis	Ezra	Ezra	Dan.	Daniel
Ex.	Exodus	Neh.	Nehemiah	Hos.	Hosea
Lev.	Leviticus	Est.	Esther	Joel	Joel
Num.	Numbers	Job	Job	Amos	Amos
Deut.	Deuteronomy	Ps./Pss.	Psalm(s)	Obad.	Obadiah
Josh.	Joshua	Prov.	Proverbs	Jonah	Jonah
Judg.	Judges	Eccl.	Ecclesiastes	Mic.	Micah
Ruth	Ruth	Song	Song of	Nah.	Nahum
1 Sam.	1 Samuel		Solomon	Hab.	Habakkuk
2 Sam.	2 Samuel	Isa.	Isaiah	Zeph.	Zephaniah
1 Kings	1 Kings	Jer.	Jeremiah	Hag.	Haggai
2 Kings	2 Kings	Lam.	Lamentations	Zech.	Zechariah
1 Chron.	1 Chronicles	Ezek.	Ezekiel	Mal.	Malachi
2 Chron.	2 Chronicles				

2. New Testament

Matt.	Matthew	Phil.	Philippians	James	James
Mark	Mark	Col.	Colossians	1 Peter	1 Peter
Luke	Luke	1 Thess.	1 Thessalonians	2 Peter	2 Peter
John	John	2 Thess.	2 Thessalonians	1 John	1 John
Acts	Acts of the	1 Tim.	1 Timothy	2 John	2 John
	Apostles	2 Tim.	2 Timothy	3 John	3 John
Rom.	Romans	Titus	Titus	Jude	Jude
1 Cor.	1 Corinthians	Philem.	Philemon	Rev.	Revelation
2 Cor.	2 Corinthians	Heb.	Hebrews		
Gal.	Galatians				
Eph.	Ephesians				

3. Bible Translations

CSB	Christian Standard Bible
ESV	English Standard Version (Text Edition 2016)
GNT	Good News Translation
NASB	New American Standard Bible
NET	The Net Bible
NIV	New International Version
NKJV	New King James Version
NLT	New Living Translation
NRSV	New Revised Standard Version
REB	The Revised English Bible

4. Other Books

BDAG	Walter Bauer, *A Greek-English Lexicon of the New Testament and Other Early Christian Literature*, 3rd ed., trans. W. F. Arndt and F. W. Gingrich, revised and edited by Frederick William Danker (Chicago: University of Chicago, 2000)
BECNT	Baker Exegetical Commentary on the New Testament
EBC	Expositor's Bible Commentary
ICC	The International Critical Commentary
IVPNTC	InterVarsity New Testament Commentary
L&N	Louw & Nida, *Greek-English Lexicon of the New Testament Based on Semantic Domains*, 2nd ed.
NICNT	New International Commentary on the New Testament
NIDNTTE	*New International Dictionary of New Testament Theology and Exegesis*, 2nd ed.
REC	Reformed Expository Commentary
TDNT	G. Kittel and G. Friedrich, eds., *Theological Dictionary of the New Testament*
TNTC	Tyndale New Testament Commentary
ZECNT	Zondervan Exegetical Commentary on the New Testament

CHAPTER 1

An Extraordinary Meeting

> *Now from Miletus he sent to Ephesus and called the elders*
> *of the church to come to him. And when they came to him,*
> *he said to them: "You yourselves know how I lived among*
> *you the whole time from the first day that*
> *I set foot in Asia." (Acts 20:17–18)*

God has given us a special gift in Paul's farewell message to the Ephesian elders. Acts 20 is a pastoral charge given by one of the greatest leaders and teachers to ever grace the Church of Jesus Christ—the apostle Paul. Timothy Keller's assessment of Paul's place in history bears repeating:

> I think it would be hard to disagree with the view that he is one of the six or seven most influential leaders in the history of the human race. One of the most influential people in history.[1]

Paul's message, recorded by Luke two thousand years ago, is as relevant today as when it was first delivered. *There is really nothing else in the New Testament comparable* to this passage. It is the only place in the New Testament in which Paul directly speaks to the church's elders, giving them their final marching orders. As Paul's parting message, it has special importance and requires our full attention.

PAUL'S MINISTRY IN EPHESUS

Paul labored as a missionary in the city of Ephesus for three years (AD 52–55). Ephesus was the third largest city in the eastern part of the Roman empire, after Alexandria of Egypt and Antioch of Syria. These years proved to be some of his most fruitful in gospel ministry. Luke comments that "all of the residents of Asia heard the word of the Lord, both Jews and Greeks" (Acts 19:10). But these were also some of the most trying years of Paul's life because he had many adversaries.

Ephesus soon became a prominent epicenter of early Christianity, next to Jerusalem, Antioch, and Rome. In Ephesus, Paul worked with a group of church leaders called "elders" or "overseers." He knew these men intimately, and they knew him. They were co-laborers together in gospel and pastoral ministry.

Initially, when Paul left Ephesus heading west to revisit his churches in Macedonia and Achaia, he had left the church in the capable hands of the Ephesian elders. At the time of their Miletus reunion (Spring, AD 57), Paul had been absent from Ephesus for over a year and a half.

After completing his work in the west, Paul headed east to Jerusalem. On the long journey, his ship stopped at the port city of Miletus. From there, Paul sent a message to Ephesus, summoning the elders of the church to come to him in Miletus for an urgent farewell meeting (Acts 20:17). Miletus was about 62 miles (100 km) from Ephesus by travel on foot.[2]

The Final Farewell Charge

But why would Paul summon the elders to Miletus, requiring them to make a long journey, just to meet with him for a short time? This meeting would be the final, face-to-face meeting where Paul would give them a final charge to emphasize what they needed to know and do in his absence. Paul's warning and exhortation is sobering:

> Pay careful attention to yourselves and to all the flock . . . I know that after my departure fierce wolves will come in among you, not sparing the flock; and from among your own selves will arise men speaking twisted things, to draw away the disciples after them. Therefore be alert. (Acts 20:28–31a)

The elders needed—as we do today—a compelling and unforgettable challenge to be faithful to their Spirit-appointed task of shepherding God's flock and guarding the gospel from false teachers.

History amply demonstrates that the truths of Paul's message cannot be overstated or repeated too often. The appalling, centuries-long failure to stop false teachers from invading churches can be traced directly back to ignorance of or disobedience to Paul's prophetic warnings to the Ephesian elders.

Any church elder who does not know the content
of Paul's message to the Ephesian elders is ill-equipped
to lead and protect God's people.

A Must-Know Passage of Scripture

Any church elder who does not know the content of Paul's message to the Ephesian elders is ill-equipped to lead and protect God's people. This will become evident as we proceed in our study. As one biblical commentator put it, this passage

> is crucial in providing for us an insight into the leadership exercised in the New Testament church, and as such, it provides for us a template by which to measure faithful oversight for the church today.[3]

I challenge you to make it your goal to master the content of Paul's prophetic, apostolic message—study it, memorize it, think deeply upon it, discuss it, teach it, and live it. If you invest the time to prayerfully study and meditate on this God-given challenge to all Christ's undershepherds, you will find warnings and exhortations essential to the task, as well as fresh motivation and divine comfort.

> Every new generation of church leaders needs
> to discover afresh Paul's instructions
> to the Ephesian elders.

Paul's instructions and pleas to the Ephesian elders are just as urgently needed today as they were that day on the shores of Miletus. Every new generation of church leaders needs to discover afresh Paul's instructions to the Ephesian elders.

Acts 20 is the Holy Spirit's summons to you to come, hear, learn, and then shepherd God's church according to God's instructions.

Initially, we should answer two important questions: Who was Paul, that we should listen to him? And who were the Ephesian elders he was speaking to?

WHO WAS PAUL?

Carefully note that out of the eighteen verses containing Paul's actual words, thirteen verses refer to his own life example. Paul presented himself as a role model for the Ephesian elders to emulate. He could speak of himself in this way without pride because he was imitating Christ and he wanted them to do the same: "Be imitators of me, as I am of Christ" (1 Cor. 11:1).

Acts 20 is a priceless treasure trove of wisdom and insight for all church leaders from Christ's chosen apostle to the Gentile nations. Paul was directly chosen by the Lord Jesus Christ to be an apostle (ἀποστολος [apostolos]), which means he was a special authorized messenger, an emissary, and an envoy directly commissioned by Christ.

Paul was not just a missionary or church planter, or a brilliant scholar—although he was all of those. Paul was Christ's unique ambassador, sent to define, defend, and proclaim the gospel to the nations.[4]

A large portion of the New Testament was written by Paul. Together with Luke his traveling companion, they wrote over fifty percent of the New Testament. Paul is the master architect of much of the vocabulary and theological concepts defining the gospel and the Church. As such, Paul played a unique role in the foundation and expansion of the Christian faith.

> Paul's gospel is Christ's gospel. What Paul teaches is what Christ teaches. What Paul commands is what Christ commands. Paul's authority to give written instructions to the churches is Christ-given authority and must be obeyed.

As Christ's ambassador, Paul did not cleverly fabricate the gospel message in his own mind. He received it by direct revelation from the risen Christ:

> For I would have you know, brothers, that the gospel that was preached by me is not man's gospel. For I did not receive it from any man, nor was I taught it, but *I received it through a revelation of Jesus Christ.* (Gal. 1:11–12)

Paul's gospel is Christ's gospel. What Paul teaches is what Christ teaches. What Paul commands is what Christ commands. *Paul's authority to give written instructions to the churches is Christ-given authority and must be obeyed.*[5] Ultimately, then, Paul's final charge to the Ephesian elders is Christ's charge, not only to the Ephesian elders, but to all undershepherds of his churches in all future generations.

WHO WERE THE EPHESIAN ELDERS?

So who were these elders from Ephesus? It is important that we answer this question accurately from Scripture. The Greek word for *elders* is *presbyteroi* (πρεσβυτεροι). Sometimes people refer to the elders as the *presbyters*, which is how we will occasionally refer to them.

The designation *elders* had already been introduced by Luke earlier in Acts to identify certain community leaders. Four different groups are referred to as elders: (1) the Jewish elders of Jerusalem, who were hostile to the Jewish Christians; (2) the Jewish elders of the Christian community in Jerusalem, who were closely associated with the twelve apostles; (3) the Christian elders appointed by Paul and Barnabas for the Gentile churches in Galatia; and (4) the Christian elders of the church in Ephesus. Speaking to the Ephesian elders, Paul makes clear that the elders are responsible for the pastoral oversight of the local church (Acts 20:28).

This New Testament concept of pastoral eldership, specifically the teaching of Acts 20, differs widely from traditional, modern-day thinking and practice. When most Christian people hear the term "elders," they think of an official church board, lay officials, influential members within the church, or temporary advisors to the senior pastor. They think of elders primarily as policymakers, financial officers, fundraisers, or administrators. I call these kinds of elders "board elders." Most people don't expect church elders to pastor the church or teach the Word. They may not even be aware that there are specific biblical qualifications for elders, including the requirement to be "able to teach" (1 Tim. 3:1–7; Titus 1:5–9).

In biblical terms, the elders are the overseers,
shepherds, stewards, teachers, and leaders
of the local church.

However, according to the New Testament, elders are to jointly lead the church, teach the Word, protect the church from false teachers, exhort the believers in sound doctrine, visit the sick, and judge doctrinal issues. In biblical terms, the elders are the overseers, shepherds, stewards, teachers, and leaders of the local church. In other words, they are the Chief Shepherd's undershepherds, held responsible for his flocks.

Since both the preeminent apostles, Paul and Peter, charge the elders—and no other person or group—to shepherd/pastor the local church, we can conclude that, in biblical terms, *the elders are responsible for the pastoral oversight of the local church* (Acts 20:28; 1 Peter 5:1–5). Biblical elders are shepherd elders or pastor elders—not board elders.

Equality and Diversity within an Eldership

From Paul's letter written to Timothy and the church at Ephesus, we learn that both equality and diversity exist within a biblical eldership (1 Tim. 5:17–18). All elders equally share the same office and pastoral charge, but at the same time the eldership will reflect a rich diversity. Obviously not all those on an elder council will be equal in giftedness, effectiveness, influence, time availability, experience, verbal skills, leadership ability, or biblical knowledge. First Timothy 5:17–18 is the key text that acknowledges diversity within the eldership council.[6]

> Let the elders who rule well be considered worthy of double honor, especially those who labor in preaching and teaching. For the Scripture says, "You shall not muzzle an ox when it treads out the grain," and, "The laborer deserves his wages." (1 Tim. 5:17–18)

Within a biblical eldership, then, there is both equality in status and a healthy diversity of giftedness and function. This allows for some elders—especially those "who labor in preaching and teaching"—to be financially supported by the church to give them more concentrated time for study and the full-time or part-time ministry of preaching and teaching.

Finally, we see from Paul's Miletus address *Paul's high view of the church elders and the indispensable nature of their work to protect and lead God's flock.* Biblical elders are not temporary, lay board members of a church. *They are the very ones the Holy Spirit of God has appointed as overseers for the purpose of shepherding the church of God (v. 28).*

Since this book is a biblical exposition of Acts 20, we will adhere to Paul's concept of elders as shepherds of God's flock. Knowing this background and context will help you better understand Paul's directives to "the elders of the church" in Ephesus.

What the Bible Says

For your own biblical preparation, study and consider each of the texts below. Let the Spirit and the Word teach you and prepare you for the rest of this study on Acts 20.

The work of elders is to:

- Lead the church of God (1 Tim. 5:17)
- Teach the people God's Word (1 Tim. 3:2; 2 Tim. 2:2; Titus 1:9)
- Equip and prepare the saints for Christian ministry (Eph. 4:11–12)
- Labor in preaching and teaching (1 Tim. 5:17)
- Guard the church from false teachers (Acts 20:28–31; Titus 1:9–10)
- Care for the church of God (1 Tim. 3:5)
- Help those within the church who are weak (Acts 20:35)
- Lay hands on certain gifted individuals (1 Tim. 4:14)
- Shepherd, that is, pastor the whole church: feed, protect, lead, and heal (Acts 20:28; 1 Peter 5:2)

- Exercise oversight: manage, supervise (1 Peter 5:2)
- Model Christian leadership (1 Peter 5:3)
- Judge doctrinal disputes (Acts 15:2–30; 16:4; 21:20–25)
- Pray for the sick and anoint them with oil (James 5:14–15)
- Handle church finances (Acts 11:29–30; 1 Peter 5:2)
- Represent the local church to other churches (Acts 11:30; 15:4, 22–23; 21:18–19)
- Be held accountable by God (Heb. 13:17)

KEY POINTS TO REMEMBER

1. Paul's authority to give written instructions to the churches is Christ-given authority and must be obeyed.

2. Acts 20 is the only passage in the New Testament in which Paul speaks directly to a church's elders, giving them a final charge.

3. Paul's message should be used both to guide current elders as to what God requires them to do in order to care effectively for his people, and to train future pastoral elders.

4. Biblical elders are responsible for the pastoral oversight of the local church.

5. Every new generation of church leaders needs to discover afresh and implement anew Paul's urgent message to the Ephesian elders.

---

[1] Timothy Keller, *The Freedom of Self-Forgetfulness: The Path to True Christian Joy* (Leyland, England: 10Publishing, 2012), 29.

[2] From the time Paul sent the messenger to Ephesus (about 62 miles or 100 km by foot) to the time of the elders' arrival would have been some eight days. For the elders, this would be a roundtrip of 124 miles or 200 km. See Eckhard J. Schnabel, *Acts*, ZECNT (Grand Rapids: Zondervan, 2012), 838.

[3] Derek W. H. Thomas, *Acts*, REC (Phillipsburg, NJ: P&R, 2011), 575.

[4] Acts 9:15–17; 20:24; 22:14–15, 21; 26:15–18; Rom. 1:1, 5, 13–14; 11:13; 15:15–18; 16:25–26; 1 Cor. 9:1–2; 11:23; 15:3–11; 2 Cor. 12:12; Gal. 1:1, 11, 16; 2:7–8; Eph. 3:1–13; 6:19–20; Phil. 1:16; Col. 1:25–27; 2 Thess. 2:15; 3:6, 14; 1 Tim. 1:11; 2:7; 2 Tim. 1:11, 13; 4:17; Titus 1:3.

[5] 2 Thess. 2:15; 2 Peter 3:15–16.

[6] If this concept is new to you, visit www.biblicaleldership.com for a free download of my 47-page booklet, *Biblical Eldership: Restoring the Eldership to Its Rightful Place in the Church.*

CHAPTER 2

Serving the Lord with All Humility

You yourselves know how I lived among you the whole time from the first day that I set foot in Asia, serving the Lord with all humility and with tears and with trials that happened to me through the plots of the Jews.
(Acts 20:18–19)

When the elders of the church in Ephesus arrived, Paul began his message by reminding them of what they already knew about his life and ministry. He said, "You yourselves know." Three times in this passage Paul directly urges the elders to remember their past experiences with him as their leader and teacher (vv. 18, 31, 34).

"How I lived among you the whole time."

Paul knew that one of the most important needs the elders had was for a Christlike role model to observe and emulate. In the end, it is example and action—not simply words—that people remember for a lifetime. So when Paul reminded the elders, "how I lived among you the whole time," *he was presenting himself as a role model of distinctive Christian leadership for them to imitate.*

Likewise, we are to study and know Paul's life and ministry so that we can follow his example.

A ROLE MODEL TO IMITATE

Like Jesus, Paul lived among the people. His life was an open book for all to read. Paul didn't ride into a city on a white horse and lecture on theology, evangelism, and church growth. He was not a classroom academic, instructing his students for a few hours a day. He was a missionary on the front line of spiritual warfare, a loving shepherd to churches and their leaders, an evangelist, a faithful man of prayer, and a *spiritual mentor to many.*

> "Paul's past ministry is understood as a resource that can help the elders face their future responsibility."
> —Robert Tannehill

For three years, from his first day in Asia until the time he left, his life was on constant display—a living, breathing example for pastoral elders to follow. He was an authentic role model of a Christlike teacher and shepherd. That is why his life has had such a lasting impact on so many people. "Paul's past ministry," writes Robert Tannehill, "is understood as a resource that can help the elders face their future responsibility."[1]

A Call to Follow

Paul understood perfectly that his life example and character was to be a model for others to imitate. In his letter to the Corinthian believers, Paul urges them to "be imitators of me." This was not an arrogant demand. Paul could say this without pride because he himself was imitating Christ, and he wanted above all else to teach all believers to imitate Christ. Helping believers to conform to the image of Christ was one of Paul's chief pastoral tasks in ministry: "that we may present everyone *mature in Christ*. For this I toil, struggling with all his energy that he powerfully works within me" (Col. 1:28–29).

Earlier in the same letter, he wrote:

> I urge you, then, *be imitators of me*. That is why I sent you Timothy, my beloved and faithful child in the Lord, to remind you of my ways in Christ, *as I teach them everywhere in every church*. (1 Cor. 4:16–17)

Paul tells the new Thessalonian believers that he and his colleagues intentionally presented themselves as "an example to imitate":

> You know what kind of men we proved to be among you for your sake. And you became imitators of us and of the Lord. (1 Thess. 1:5–6)

> For you yourselves know how you ought to imitate us . . . It was not because we do not have that right [to financial support], but to give you in ourselves *an example to imitate*. (2 Thess. 3:7–9)

To his dear friends in the city of Philippi he wrote:

> Brothers, *join in imitating me*, and keep your eyes on those who walk according to the example you have in us. (Phil. 3:17)

> What you have learned and received and heard and seen *in me*—practice these things. (Phil. 4:9)

Paul also called on his young assistants to be role models for others to follow:

> Let no one despise you for your youth, but *set the believers an example* in speech, in conduct, in love, in faith, in purity. (1 Tim. 4:12; also Titus 2:7–8)

Just as Paul had done, the writer of Hebrews instructed his readers to imitate the faith of their leaders:

> Remember your leaders, those who spoke to you the word of God. Consider the outcome of their way of life, and *imitate their faith.* (Heb. 13:7; see also Heb. 6:12)

You should always be mindful that people are watching you as you serve the Lord, some of whom are younger men who will be the next generation of pastoral elders.

Imitate Their Faith, not Their Clothes

As the last two passages demonstrate, by the term "imitate" both the writer of Hebrews and Paul do not mean exact duplication. Imitating Paul doesn't mean having to speak Aramaic, wear sandals and a toga, eat figs, or ride on a donkey. Rather they are calling others to imitate their faith, their love, their self-sacrifice, and their pattern of life and behavior.

While I was sitting in a restaurant with friends, twelve men walked in dressed like Jesus with sandals, robes, long hair, beards, speaking in old Elizabethan, King James English, and walking, not driving by car. The whole thing looked comical. They thought that following Jesus meant wearing Jesus-like clothes and having a Jesus-like beard. They didn't seem to remember that Jesus warned his disciples of the subtle danger of trusting in outward religious appearances, and not the inner heart condition before God.[2]

Seeing Christ in Paul

The Ephesian presbyters had the extraordinary privilege of seeing Christ in Paul. Now Paul expected them—and us—to replicate what they learned from him about humbly serving Christ and sacrificially caring for his people. "What you have learned and received and heard and seen in me—practice these things" (Phil. 4:9).

Like his Master, Paul was saying to the elders, "Follow me and I will make you fishers of men and shepherds of people." Paul led by example. And he would remind us today to *never underestimate the extraordinary power of your personal life example to influence and inspire other people positively for God.*

A HUMBLE SLAVE OF THE LORD JESUS CHRIST

Paul called upon his beloved friends to remember his life example. But how did he live among them? What did his life look like? Here is his answer: "From the first day that I set foot in Asia, [I served] the Lord with all humility and with tears and trials that happened to me through the plots of the Jews" (vv. 18–19). Note that Paul does not rehearse his many successes, expansive travels, brilliant intellect, indomitable zeal, heavenly visions, extraordinary miracles, or divine authority. Instead, *the first thing he mentions is his humble service to the Lord Jesus Christ.* This is very interesting. What he says here sets the tone for the rest of the address.

Serving the Lord as His Slave

The Greek verb for "serving" is the verb for "serving as a slave" (δουλεύω [*douleuō*]). In some of his letters Paul referred to himself as a "slave" (δοῦλος [*doulos*]) of the Lord Jesus.[3] From the time of his life-transforming encounter with the risen Christ on the Damascus road, Paul preached that "Jesus is Lord":

> For what we proclaim is not ourselves, but *Jesus Christ as Lord*, with ourselves as *your servants* [lit. slaves] for Jesus' sake. (2 Cor. 4:5)

Paul understood that he had been purchased by, and therefore was now owned by, the Lord Jesus Christ. He could gladly say, "Christ Jesus has made me his own" (Phil. 3:12). Paul was not his own master; he was a willing and joyous slave of the Lord Jesus. All that Paul did in Ephesus can be summarized as "serving the Lord." Indeed, his whole life was spent serving the Lord, and whom better to serve than our Lord and Savior Jesus Christ?

Are You a Slave of the Lord Jesus Christ?

Do you view your life and ministry as humble, slave-like service to your Lord and Master, Jesus Christ? You should! The Scripture says, "You are not your own, for you were bought with a price. So glorify God in your body" (1 Cor. 6:19–20). For the believer, the truth is:

> None of us lives to himself, and none of us dies to himself. For if we live, *we live to the Lord*, and if we die, we die to the Lord. So then, whether we live or whether we die, *we are the Lord's*. For to this end Christ died and lived again, that he might be Lord both of the dead and of the living. (Rom. 14:7–9)

The best elders are those who see themselves as slaves of the Lord Jesus Christ, appointed by him and entrusted with the care of his blood-bought people.

Humility permeated his actions, his words, his attitudes, his teaching, his interactions with his fellow workers, and his leader-follower relationships.

Serving the Lord with All Humility

Paul served the Lord "with all humility." That is the only acceptable way to serve the Lord, and the only proper attitude of a slave. Humility is a distinctive Christian virtue.

Humility is the key to understanding Paul's character and leadership style. In a world super-saturated with ugly pride and selfish ambition, Paul served the Lord with "all" humility.[4] Humility permeated his actions, his words, his attitudes, and his teaching. It could be observed in his interactions with his fellow workers, and his leader-follower relationships.

Learning from Jesus

All that Paul knew about humility and self-sacrificial servanthood he learned from the Perfect Servant, the one who "humbled himself" and "made himself nothing, taking the form of a slave" (Phil 2:5–8).

Jesus turned the leadership pyramid upside down.
The leader is servant of all, not the boss of all!

Paul learned about humility from Jesus's repeated teaching on "greatness" and being "first" in the kingdom of God. *Jesus's redefinition of greatness and leadership status governed Paul's entire ministry style.* Jesus warned his followers repeatedly not to conform to the world's ideas and practices of status, power, and authority. Jesus turned the leadership pyramid upside down. The leader is servant of all, not the boss of all!

One very remarkable lesson Paul would have learned from his "Teacher and Lord" is that a Christlike leader should be prepared to humbly stoop and wash the dirty feet of others, just as a slave would do:

Do you understand what I have done to you? You call me Teacher and Lord, and you are right, for so I am. If I then, your Lord and Teacher, have washed your feet, you also ought to wash one another's feet. For I have given you an example, that *you also should do just as I have done to you.* (John 13:12–15)

The unforgettable example of Jesus stooping to wash the disciples' feet teaches us that,

The symbol of an authentically Christian leadership is not the purple robe of an emperor, but the coarse apron of a slave; not a throne of ivory and gold, but a basin of water for the washing of feet.[5]

Insights into the Humble Mind of a Servant of God

Paul, the once proud, young Pharisee, became a humble man under the lordship of Jesus Christ. He knew that all of his brilliant gifting was a result of God's grace. He knew that his success in the gospel came from the strength the Lord provided. He felt deeply how undeserving he was to even be an apostle of Christ: "For I am the least of the apostles, unworthy to be called an apostle" (1 Cor. 15:9).

Lowly-Mindedness: Paul correctly understood his insignificance and smallness in relation to God's infinite greatness, his unworthiness before God's absolute holiness, and his utter dependence on God for everything: "But our sufficiency is from God, who has made us sufficient to be ministers of a new covenant" (2 Cor. 3:5–6). Only with the humble is there the fear of God and thus the beginning of knowledge and wisdom. "With the humble is wisdom" (Prov. 11:2).

With a proper estimate of himself and a genuine sincerity of heart he could say, "I am nothing" (2 Cor. 12:11), because Christ is everything. Thus, he gladly subordinated himself under the mighty hand of God and of Christ. There is no false humility here.

All by Grace: Paul knew that "by the grace of God I am what I am" (1 Cor. 15:10). Elsewhere he says, "To me, though I am the very least of all the saints, this grace was given" (Eph. 3:8). He viewed himself and his colleagues as "jars of clay," fragile vessels carrying the living water of the gospel (2 Cor. 4:7). *He wanted people to view himself and his fellow workers as "servants through whom" they had believed,* and "servants of Christ and stewards of the mysteries of God" (1 Cor. 3:5; 4:1).

The Virtues of a Humble Leader

Paul was a strong but humble man imitating Christ's humility. *If you cannot imagine how a strong, gifted, brilliant, energetic leader can also be a loving, humble servant, consider carefully the life of Paul.*

Paul was self-effacing, modest, and selfless. He was others-oriented, even willing to do manual work with his own hands to support himself and to help others. He lived what scholars call the "cruciform life," which means a life shaped by the cross of Christ (Phil. 3:10).

A Christlike humble attitude makes a leader more teachable, more approachable, and more receptive to constructive criticism. It makes him better able to see his own limitations and failures, better able to submit to and work with others, and better qualified to deal with the sins and failures of other people.

A humble leader is less defensive, less prone to fight, quicker to reconcile differences, and more at ease in personal relationships. A humble soul enjoys promoting the gifts and popularity of others, and is not jealous or envious of others' accomplishments. Only with an attitude of "all humility" can you lead in a Jesus-like way.

The Glue: *The local church is a highly relational, close-knit community of brothers and sisters all indwelt by the Holy Spirit of God.* It is not a top-down community led by one person with full authority to govern. In a highly relational community of brothers and sisters the virtue of humility (and love) is the glue that holds people together and enables them to resolve the natural disagreements that occur between people.

> If you cannot imagine how a strong, gifted, brilliant, energetic leader can also be a loving, humble servant, consider carefully the life of Paul.

THE DIOTREPHES-LIKE LEADER

Paul was nothing like the arrogant church leader Diotrephes, who liked "to put himself first" (3 John 9). He could not say as Paul did, *I served the Lord and his people with all humility.*

Diotrephes is the classic, autocratic church leader, the strong man, the narcissistic pastor who builds the church around himself. *He represents the dark side of Christian leadership.* The aged apostle John described him this way:

> I have written something to the church, but Diotrephes, *who likes to put himself first*, does not acknowledge our authority. So if I [John] come, I will bring up what he is doing, talking wicked nonsense against us. And not content with that, he refuses to welcome the brothers, and also stops those who want to and puts them out of the church. (3 John 9–10)

Diotrephes thought so highly of himself that he even criticized and refused to listen to the beloved apostle John. He did not submit to apostolic authority.

Diotrephes was an intimidating leader, creating an atmosphere of fear and guilt, demanding unconditional loyalty. To those who followed him and agreed with him, I imagine he was a charming, gifted, strong authority figure. This fit well within the highly stratified Greco-Roman culture that prized strong, dominating leaders.

Diotrephes clearly was not a builder of people but a limiter. He was not a uniter but a divider. He was not a promoter of others but a self-promoter. He was not a humble-minded leader; he was a competitive leader. He would not share the ministry with peers and colleagues as did Paul. Like all proud men, he refused godly correction and instruction. His heart was not contrite before God, and his arrogant spirit divided and hurt people. In Paul's view, he was "a noisy gong or a clanging cymbal" (1 Cor. 13:1).

Redeeming Leadership from the World

Diotrephes is the Bible's example of what a Christian leader is *not* to be like. He represents the world's strong-man model, sitting at the top of the leadership pyramid.

Jesus radically challenged the prevailing leadership values of both the religious and secular leaders of his day. Luke records that,

> A dispute also arose among them, as to which of them was to be regarded as the greatest. And he said to them, "The kings of the Gentiles exercise lordship over them, and those in authority over them are called benefactors. But not so with you. Rather, let the greatest among you become as the youngest, and *the leader as the one who serves*. For who is the greater, one who reclines at table or one who serves? Is it not the one who reclines at table? But I am among you as the one who serves." (Luke 22:24–27)[6]

The Jesus-style of leadership means leading others, not lording one's authority over others. It is an others-oriented style of leadership, where the leader serves the people—even the most insignificant ones—and expects nothing in return. It is loving attentiveness to other people's needs, marked by suffering for the good of others, even being willing to die for others. It is denying self and sacrificing oneself for others; it is promoting and advancing others. It is being a Philippians 2 leader.[7]

Charles Colson experienced worldly power and high position as Special Counsel to the President of the United States, and later became a born-again, Bible-believing Christian. He skillfully describes the differences between the worldly view of power and the biblical view:

> Nothing distinguishes the kingdoms of man from the Kingdom of God more than their diametrically opposed views of the exercise of power. One seeks to control people, the other to serve people; one promotes self, the other prostrates self; the one seeks prestige and position, the other lifts up the lowly and despised.[8]

To Be Clear: Jesus did not deny the need for positions of leadership, the exercise of human authority, the pursuit of greatness, or excellence in leadership. To those who have the spiritual gift of leadership, Paul says lead "with zeal" (Rom. 12:8). What Jesus taught was that in his kingdom and under his lordship the exercise of leadership and authority must be of a different kind from the self-promoting, patron-client model of his day.

STILL A PROBLEM

In reminding the Ephesian elders that he served the Lord with "all humility," Paul was also at the same time warning them of *the universal temptations that church leaders face—pride of position, pride of title, pride of knowledge, and pride of giftedness.* "Pride is without doubt, the chief occupational hazard of the preacher," remarks John Stott.[9] Despite the fact that humility and servanthood are central to Jesus's teaching on leadership and community life, the lack of humility among Christian leaders is still acknowledged as a widespread problem.

At the third Lausanne Congress in Cape Town, South Africa (2010), the 5,000 plus representatives from every country in the world agreed that lack of humility among pastors was a worldwide harm to believers spiritually and needed to be urgently addressed.[10]

What the People Want

Unfortunately, we have to acknowledge that a strong autocratic style of leadership is often outwardly successful and popular with people. Many people want to follow a strong-man leader, a Diotrephes-like figure, a man they deem anointed by God with power to rule. They want the tough-minded, singular leadership style of the world.

This was certainly true of the Corinthian believers. Paul didn't match up to their Greco-Roman concept of the strong-man leader, thus the Corinthians became easy prey for the so-called "super apostles" who misled and abused them:

> For you gladly bear with fools, being wise yourselves! For you bear it if someone makes slaves of you, or devours you, or takes advantage of you, or puts on airs, or strikes you in the face. To my shame, I must say, we were too weak for that! (2 Cor. 11:19–21)

To some of the Christians Paul seems weak and unimpressive, certainly not great or first in status. They may have thought, as some do today, that the concept of "servant-leader" is a contradiction of terms and not really a practical, workable leadership concept.

Failure to Obey: Despite the repeated teachings of Jesus and Paul on (1) humility, (2) love, (3) brotherhood, and (4) servanthood, those truths were and are often ignored. After the first century and beyond, most churches gradually adopted the Greco-Roman hierarchical patterns of status and power for its leaders and community structure. An unscriptural clerical and priestly caste arose that was obsessed with personal titles, clothes, status, and power.

> Only those who exhibit Christlike humility,
> servanthood, brotherhood, and love are truly
> great in God's eyes and first in his kingdom.

What God Wants

Contrary to the natural ways of this world, according to Jesus and Paul, only those elders who are loving, humble servants can genuinely manifest the incomparable life of Jesus Christ to their congregations and a watching world. Only those who exhibit Christlike humility, servanthood, brotherhood, and love are truly great in God's eyes and first in his kingdom.

Make it your aim to serve the Lord as his slave with all humility of mind! *This is Paul's first self-description that he wants pastoral elders to emulate.*

Helpful Resources

To see how radically countercultural Jesus's teaching on leadership, greatness, status, and power is, as well as Paul's humble life and leadership styles, read Joseph H. Hellerman's book *Embracing Shared Ministry: Power and Status in the Early Church and Why It Matters Today* (Grand Rapids: Kregel, 2013). This book is a must read.

To grasp how servant leadership would handle difficult church situations, read Alexander Strauch and Robert L. Peterson, *Agape Leadership: Lessons in Spiritual Leadership from the Life of R. C. Chapman* (Littleton: Lewis and Roth, 1991). It is a short, eighty-page booklet.

KEY POINTS TO REMEMBER

1. Never underestimate the extraordinary power of your personal life example to inspire other people positively for God.

---

2. See yourself as a willing bondslave of the Lord Jesus Christ.

3. If you cannot imagine how a strong, gifted, brilliant, energetic leader can also be a humble servant, consider carefully the life of Paul.

4. A humble attitude makes a leader more teachable, more approachable, better able to submit to and work with others, and less defensive, less prone to fight, quicker to reconcile differences, and more at ease in personal relationships.

---

[1] Robert Tannehill, *The Narrative Unity of Luke-Acts: A Literary Interpretation, Volume 2: The Acts of the Apostle* (Fortress Press, 1990), 253.

[2] Matt. 6:1–18; 23:1–12; Mark 7:1–12.

[3] Rom. 1:1; 1 Cor. 7:22; 2 Cor. 4:5; Gal. 1:10; Phil. 1:1; Titus 1:1.

[4] BDAG, s.v. "ταπεινοφροσύνη," 989, "humility, modesty"; see Eph. 4:2; Phil. 2:3; Col. 3:12; 1 Peter 5:5. See *NIDNTTE*, s.v. "ταπεινός," 4:448–454; Walter Grundmann, s.v. "ταπεινός," in *TDNT*, 8:1–26.

[5] John R. W. Stott, *The Cross of Christ* (Downers Grove: InterVarsity, 1986), 288.

[6] Read also Matt. 11:29; 20:20–28 [=Mark 10:35–45]; 23:5–12; Mark 9:33–35; Luke 14:7–11; John 13:3–17.

[7] *"Do nothing from selfish ambition or conceit, but in humility count others more significant than yourselves. Let each of you look not only to his own interests, but also to the interests of others. Have this mind among yourselves, which is yours in Christ Jesus"* (Phil. 2:3–5).

Here Paul contrasts "selfish ambition" and "conceit" with "humility." According to the text, humility involves counting other people "more significant than" yourself and considering not just your "own interests," but also the interests and advantages of other people. Jesus Christ is the supreme example of humility and self-sacrificing service to others.

[8] Charles Colson, *Kingdoms in Conflict* (Grand Rapids: Zondervan, 1987), 274.

[9] John R. W. Stott, *Between Two Worlds: The Art of Preaching in the Twentieth Century* (Grand Rapids: Eerdmans, 1982), 320.

[10] *The Cape Town Commitment: A Confession of Faith and a Call to Action* (Bodmin, UK: The Lausanne Movement, 2011); *The Lausanne Legacy: Landmarks in Global Mission* (Peabody, MA: Hendrickson, 2016).

CHAPTER 3

Serving the Lord Amidst Tears and Persecution

You yourselves know how I lived among you the whole time
from the first day that I set foot in Asia, serving the Lord with
all humility and with tears and with trials that happened to
me through the plots of the Jews.
(Acts 20:18–19)

Paul began his farewell message by reminding the Ephesian elders of how he had served the Lord with "all humility" the whole time he was with them. A humble spirit characterized Paul's life and ministry. This same spirit of humility must now manifest itself in the elders' lives and ministry.

Paul also reminded them of how he served the Lord "with tears and with trials that happened to me through the plots of the Jews." By recounting his personal experiences of tears and trials, *he sought to prepare the elders for the heartaches and persecutions they also would inevitably face.*

Like Jesus, Paul was a deeply empathetic man.

SERVING THE LORD WITH TEARS

Like Jesus, Paul wept. Like Jesus, Paul had a compassionate heart. Like Jesus, Paul gave his life for the sheep. He was a shepherd leader full of "the affection of Christ Jesus" for his converts (Phil. 1:8). Paul knew what it was to "weep with those who weep" (Rom. 12:15). *Like Jesus, Paul was a deeply empathetic man.*

Empathy is such an important virtue for a church elder. Empathy is "the ability to identify with and understand another person's feelings or difficulties."[1] "Who is weak, and I am not weak?" says Paul. "Who is made to fall, and I am not indignant?" (2 Cor. 11:29).

Paul was not an aloof, unemotional leader. He was not emotionally detached from people. He was not like the hired shepherd, serving only when paid for his efforts. No! Never!

Paul loved those in his charge, even when they were difficult to deal with. To the Corinthian believers, who caused him many heartaches and sleepless nights, he wrote: "You are in our hearts, to die together and to live together" (2 Cor. 7:3). Later in the same letter he says, "I seek not what is yours but you. . . . I will most gladly spend and be spent for your souls" (2 Cor. 12:14–15).

The Tears Caused by False Teachers and Wayward Converts

Paul wept over the false teachers' unrelenting attacks on the gospel and his children in the faith: "For many, of whom I have often told you and now tell you even *with tears,* walk as enemies of the cross of Christ" (Phil. 3:18).

Tears of Anguish: It was with tears that Paul repeatedly warned the Ephesian elders of savage wolves seeking to divide and devour the flock: "Therefore be alert, remembering that for three years I did not cease night or day to admonish every one *with tears*" (Acts 20:31). Seeing God's sheep torn to pieces by wolves caused him much anguish of soul.

Pastoral Tears: Paul's conflicts with the independent-minded Corinthians caused him intense emotional pain and tears:

> For I wrote to you out of much affliction and anguish of heart and with many tears, not to cause you pain but to let you know the abundant love that I have for you. (2 Cor. 2:4; see also 2 Cor. 12:21)

Parting Tears: After Paul's speech, Luke recorded that there was "much weeping on the part of all; they embraced Paul and kissed him" (Acts 20:37). Such an outpouring of emotion seems to have been a common experience at such farewells (2 Tim. 1:4). Tears marked Paul's service for the Lord, and deep affection characterized his personal relationships with converts and fellow workers in the gospel.

Be Prepared for Tears

When you love people and are attentive to their needs, you also will weep over the many heartaches, conflicts, and hardships they face. You will weep over broken marriages, divided homes, ugly conflicts among church members, untimely deaths, crippling sicknesses, and dreadful addictions to pornography, alcohol, or drugs. Like the weeping prophet Jeremiah, you too will weep over people's foolish idols and senseless rebellion against God's wise instructions.

Dealing with People's Sins: One tear-filled situation I will never forget was having to deal with a fellow elder and older friend who was living in adultery but doing everything in his power to deny it. For nearly a year, we elders had to face his angry denials, clever lies, intimidations, threats of lawsuits, and false accusations against the church's discipline.

As you might expect, some people sided with the sinning brother, claiming we were falsely accusing him, while others supported the elders. Families and friends were divided with different opinions, angrily taking sides. At times, it seemed the church would break apart.

The stresses were overwhelming, leading to many sleepless nights. For many months I couldn't help but mull over the details of the situation and the cruel things people were saying—people who didn't have all the facts or were fooled by the man's bold-faced lies and charismatic personality.

Even individuals and Christian organizations outside of our church got involved in attacking the elders. The whole thing was a mess, but my fellow elders and I were confident that we had done the right thing for the church, for the sinning brother, and for his family by removing him from the church in discipline as the Lord commanded: "Purge the evil person from among you" (1 Cor. 5:13; also Matt. 18:17).

In this case, eight years after he was disfellowshipped from the church, this brother came to us broken and repentant, humbly seeking restoration and reconciliation. The truth was told, the repentance was real, and our fellowship with him was restored by God's grace. This too was a cause for tears, but now they were tears of joy.

High Emotional Stress: In this sin-saturated world we will experience many heartbreaks and tears. Only in heaven will all tears be wiped away forever. But for now, there is a deeply emotional toll that goes along with the work of shepherding God's people. We are not building computers or designing websites. We are dealing with beloved family members, brothers and sisters in Christ, and the priceless message of eternal salvation through Jesus's death and resurrection. The stakes are high, the hurts run deep, and the stress can be unrelenting at times.

Without the empowering presence of the Holy Spirit
to do the work of shepherding people, such intimate
exposure to people's inner problems and sins
can crush a person emotionally.

Even if you are not a person who weeps easily, you will experience grief, emotional distress, anguish of mind, and sleepless nights. *The heavy burdens of people's sins will weigh on your mind daily.* Without the empowering presence of the Holy Spirit[2] to do the work of shepherding, such intimate exposure to people's inner problems and sins can crush a person emotionally. So prepare yourself by opening your eyes to the harsh realities ahead as you shepherd God's flock through the cursed wilderness of this world. As a friend of mine often says, "The fingerprints of the curse are on everything."

Deeply Meaningful Work

Yes, there are tears and heartaches in store for the shepherds of God's people. But I must say, there is also great joy and profound personal fulfillment in caring for God's people. The joys outweigh the heartaches. This is true because the task of shepherding people involves matters of eternal consequence.

In caring for God's flock, there is a strong sense of doing the will of God and pleasing the Lord Jesus Christ. For the believer, nothing is more meaningful and rewarding than that:

> So whether we are at home [in the body] or away [in heaven], *we make it our aim to please him* [Christ]. For we must all appear before the judgment seat of Christ. (2 Cor. 5:9–10)

Also, keep in mind that the "chief Shepherd" knows perfectly what you are suffering, and he sees each tear you shed for his people. He has promised all his undershepherds that at his appearing, "You will receive the unfading crown of glory" (1 Peter 5:4). Our Lord is no man's debtor. He superabundantly rewards his servants. You and I will receive much more than we ever deserve for our labors.

SERVING THE LORD AMIDST PERSECUTION

Since the day Cain killed his godly brother Abel, this world and the god of this world have been at war with God, his prophets, his people, and his Messiah. This is the oldest continuous war on the planet. It is between the seed of the woman and the seed of the serpent (Gen. 3:15).

> "If the world hates you, know that it has hated me before it hated you. . . . If they persecuted me, they will also persecute you." John 15:18–20

From personal experience, King David knew the hatred of the pagan nations for God's law and his anointed ruler:

> Why do the nations rage and the peoples plot in vain? The kings of the earth set themselves, and the rulers take counsel together, against the Lord and against his Anointed, saying, "Let us burst their bonds apart and cast away their cords from us." (Ps. 2:1–3)

Jesus also knew what it was to be hated by this world. He was the suffering Messiah. As the prophet Isaiah predicted, "He was despised and rejected by men, a man of sorrows and acquainted with grief" (Isa. 53:3). The four Gospels all describe how Jesus was utterly despised, rejected, and finally crucified on a Roman cross.

Even before his crucifixion, Jesus suffered the worst humiliation imaginable. At the hands of the religious leaders, he was arrested and falsely tried as a criminal worthy of death. They spat in his face and, while he was blindfolded, they punched him, demanding that he prophesy who hit him. Roman soldiers clothed him with a purple robe and a crown made of thorns and mockingly bowed down before him, hailing him as the king of the Jews; they savagely beat on his head with a reed; they flogged him with a whip, and then they led him out to be publicly displayed before the religious leaders of Israel. At this most ignominious and horrifying sight, the rulers of the nation cried out in utter hatred: "Away with him, away with him, crucify him!" (John 19:15). Jesus was then forced to carry his own heavy cross through the city streets to the place of execution. And even once he was upon the cross, the soldiers and religious leaders continued to mock and humiliate him.

Jonathan Edwards vividly captures this vehement hatred of Christ by the people:

> When once God became man, and came down to dwell here, among such vipers as fallen men, they hated and persecuted him. . . . Nothing would do, but he must be put to death. All cry out. Crucify him, crucify him. Away with him. They had rather Barabbas, who greatly deserved death, should live, than he should die. Nothing would restrain them from it; even all his preaching, and all his miracles: but they would kill him. And it was not the ordinary kind of execution that would satisfy them; but it must be the most cruel, and most ignominious they possibly could invent. And they aggravated it as much as they could, by mocking him, and spitting on him, and scourging him. This shows what the nature and tendency of man's enmity with God is; here it appeared in its true colors.[3]

Jesus could not have been clearer when he warned his disciples: "If the world hates you, know that it has hated me before it hated you. . . . *If they persecuted me, they will also persecute you*" (John 15:18–20). The entire book of Acts illustrates the truth of Jesus's warnings. The first Christians were threatened and arrested by local authorities, suffering beatings, slanderous accusations, expulsion from cities, court appearances, and executions.

This hatred for Christ's message and his messengers was demonstrated most dramatically by the Sanhedrin (the Supreme Court of Israel) against the twelve apostles during the first days of the Christian era. Luke records: "They were enraged and wanted to kill them [the apostles]" because of their irrefutable witness of the risen Messiah (Acts 5:33).

> That same hate-filled anger is directed to anyone today who would proclaim the biblical gospel of a crucified Savior, risen from the dead and coming back again to judge the world.

Again we see this hate-filled wrath unleashed against Stephen as he tried to defend the gospel before the Sanhedrin: "But they cried out with a loud voice and stopped their ears and rushed together at him. Then they cast him out of the city and stoned him" (Acts 7:57–58).

Today that same hate-filled anger is directed to anyone who would proclaim the biblical gospel of a crucified Savior, risen from the dead and coming back again to judge the world. Ultimately this scorn and hostility against Christians is Satan's hate-filled fury against Christ and his redeemed people.

Although Acts tells the exciting story of the advancement of the gospel into the Gentile world, it also spells out plainly the concurrent resistance and hostility to God's message and messengers. *This world is at war with its Creator and with all who align themselves with Christ.* So we must, as Paul writes, be prepared for intense spiritual warfare:

> Put on the whole armor of God, that you may be able to stand against the schemes of the devil. For we do not wrestle against flesh and blood, but against the rulers, against the authorities, against the cosmic powers over this present darkness, against the spiritual forces of evil in the heavenly places. (Eph. 6:11–12)

Plots on Paul's Life

For Paul, serving the Lord was also marked by trials that consisted largely of persecution by his fellow Jews. Paul speaks from a life that experienced deep suffering and cruel persecution.

In verse 19 Paul emphasizes his trials from the "plots of the Jews." These were organized, planned conspiracies to kill Paul. They were instigated and carried out by the very ones who professed to know the God of the Old Testament and to be his covenant people. This made the persecution all the more personal for Paul. There was persecution from other sources, but the unbelieving Jews especially despised Paul's message of a crucified, risen Messiah and of salvation for both Jews and Gentiles by grace through faith. The bitter hatred from his fellow Jews was among Paul's severest trials.

So hateful were these religious authorities toward Paul and his gospel—and ultimately of Christ—that on one occasion more than forty men bound themselves in "an oath neither to eat nor drink till they had killed Paul" (Acts 23:12–35). This unlawful plot was made in agreement with the highest Jewish officials, the chief priests, and elders. If it were not for divine intervention by Roman soldiers, Paul would have been brutally murdered by his fellow countrymen.

His Jewish opponents considered Paul an egregious traitor of God's law and their sacred traditions, who rightly deserved death. Once while he was in Jerusalem in the temple area, the Jewish worshippers brutally attacked him, crying out, "Away with such a fellow from the earth! For he should not be allowed to live" (Acts 22:22).

The First Targets of Persecution

Since the days of the apostles, the world has not been gospel- or Christ-friendly. Persecution of Paul began immediately after his conversion on the Damascus Road and followed him like a hungry lion until he was finally martyred in Rome under the Emperor

Nero. *Suffering for the gospel was an integral part of his apostleship[4] and his special identification with Christ in his sufferings and death.*

By reminding the elders of his own trials
by persecution, Paul was preparing the elders
to face organized, planned persecution
by determined adversaries.

While Paul was at Ephesus, he was the bull's-eye for the flaming darts of persecution. But now that he had left, he knew the church's leaders would be the chief targets of the devil's torments. By reminding the elders of his own trials by persecution, *Paul was preparing the elders to face organized, planned persecution by determined adversaries.*

State-Controlled Opposition: If you live in a country where the government (or state religion) can openly persecute Christians, you already know that church leaders are the first to be slated for attack. The enemies of the gospel know that if they eliminate the shepherds, the flocks will scatter in fear. As a result of Stephen's public death by stoning and Saul's ruthless persecutions, the believers in Jerusalem "scattered" (Acts 7:58–8:3).

Even today persecution can be horribly violent, as was the 2015 execution of twenty-one Egyptian Christians working in Libya. They were made to kneel on the ground in front of cameras and were ordered to denounce their faith in Jesus Christ. When they all refused, they were summarily beheaded by agents of the radical Islamic State. Their gruesome deaths were filmed and broadcast around the world.

Secular Society's Opposition: If you live in a democratic, secular-ized society, you will not be tortured, killed, or put in a concentra-tion camp. But you will be discriminated against, verbally ridiculed, threatened with lawsuits, or labeled an intolerant bigot. Your neighbors may not want to associate with you or even speak to you. You may be accused of "misinterpreting Jesus's beautiful message of love, tolerance, inclusivism, social justice, and world peace."

Such persecution can be very subtle. C. S. Lewis was a Fellow (a tutor or instructor) at Oxford University for twenty-one years. In the normal course of events he would have been granted a professorship, but he was repeatedly passed over for such a promotion. His opponents offered a number of excuses, but the true reason was his outspoken Christianity.

One scholar explained his opposition by saying Lewis had written *The Screwtape Letters*, a book ironically about the wiles of the devil. Another told A. N. Wilson (Lewis' biographer) that Lewis was "the most evil man he had ever met." When asked to explain, he said that Lewis believed in God and used his "cleverness to corrupt the young."[5]

Our biblical worldview on God, Scripture, truth, gender, abortion, and marriage is totally unacceptable to modern thinking. Our beliefs will be bitterly opposed and considered "hate speech." Our Christian values are scorned by the general public, and labeled as something from the Dark Ages and grossly offensive.

As our Western societies become more godless and secularized, expect opposition to escalate. This is already happening in certain countries. A new, more aggressive, hostile secularism has emerged in recent years. Proponents of this new, militant secularism are intolerant of historic Christian teaching. They are determined to silence biblical Christianity by even passing laws that will criminalize certain Christian beliefs.

Ample Warnings

Jesus's earliest followers were cautioned repeatedly that they should expect opposition to their faith. Paul reminded the afflicted believers in the city of Thessalonica that Christians were "destined for this":

That no one be moved by these afflictions. For you yourselves know that we are destined for this. For when we were with you, we kept telling you beforehand that we were to suffer affliction, just as it has come to pass, and just as you know. (1 Thess. 3:3–4)

On this text, John Stott commented, "It is very interesting to learn that a regular topic of Paul's instruction to converts was the inevitability of suffering."[6]

Paul consistently included this emphasis whenever he taught or wrote to the first-generation believers:

Through many tribulations we must enter the kingdom of God. (Acts 14:22)

Striving side by side for the faith of the gospel, and not frightened in anything by your opponents. . . . For it has been granted to you ["graciously given"[7]] that for the sake of Christ you should not only believe in him but also *suffer for his sake*. (Phil. 1:27–29)

All who desire to live a godly life in Christ Jesus *will be persecuted*. (2 Tim. 3:12)

"It is very interesting to learn that a regular topic of Paul's instruction to converts was the inevitability of suffering." —John Stott

Similarly, the apostles John and Peter warned those to whom they wrote:

Do not be surprised, brothers, that the world hates you. (1 John 3:13)

Beloved, do not be surprised at the fiery trial when it comes upon you to test you, as though something strange were happening to you. (1 Peter 4:12)

Rejoice and Look Heavenward: Whatever persecution or ridicule we face in life because of our faith, Jesus urges us to look to our glorious future rewards:

Blessed are you when others revile you and persecute you and utter all kinds of evil against you falsely on my account. *Rejoice and be glad, for your reward is great in heaven,* for so they persecuted the prophets who were before you. (Matt. 5:11–12)

And so does Peter:

Rejoice insofar as you share Christ's sufferings, that you may also rejoice and be glad when his glory is revealed. If you are insulted for the name of Christ, *you are blessed, because the Spirit of glory and of God rests upon you.* (1 Peter 4:13–14)

PREPARE YOURSELF AND OTHERS FOR PERSECUTION

In recent years, persecutions and martyrdoms of Christians have increased worldwide. Religious terrorist groups have killed thousands of Christian believers in Africa and India. *Therefore, you need to prepare yourselves and others to suffer for the gospel.* Don't be caught off guard, "knowing that the same kinds of suffering are being experienced by your brotherhood throughout the world" (1 Peter 5:9; see also Rev. 6:9–11).

You need to prepare yourselves and others to suffer for the gospel. Don't be caught off guard.

It is frightening and traumatizing to be verbally ridiculed or physically assaulted by relatives, neighbors, or government officials. Most people cannot withstand hostile persecution emotionally. Some will even turn away from the faith to avoid suffering and persecution (see Luke 8:13). So they will need strong community support and spiritual guidance from biblically-minded shepherds. *This means you need to be prepared to teach them God's perspective on suffering for the name of Christ.*

But how do you prepare yourself and others for persecution? Focus on exactly what the Scriptures teach about suffering for Christ and the gospel. The New Testament has a remarkable amount of material about persecution and suffering—much more than you might realize.

Below are some of the major biblical claims about suffering persecution. You will find that your theology, and especially your eschatology (the doctrine of last things), determine your attitude and responses to persecution.

As you study Scripture on this subject, God's Word will remove any unrealistic, idealized expectations about life as a Christian in a Christ-rejecting world. Instead it will give you future hope, direction, and immense encouragement. *Be prepared to teach these truths to others and especially to your young people.* For the Scripture references and full citations for each of these points, go to www.Acts20book.com.

- Jesus is the supreme example of suffering
  at the hands of sinners.
- Jesus predicted the inevitability of persecution.
- The apostles predicted the inevitability of persecution.
- Satan instigates persecution against believers.
- Suffering is a part of gospel ministry in a Christ-
  rejecting world.
- Suffering for the gospel is participation in Christ's sufferings.

- Sharing in Christ's sufferings is matched by sharing in Christ's encouragement and comfort.
- Persecution tests the genuineness of our faith.
- Suffering for the gospel builds stable character.
- We are cursed by the world, but blessed by God.
- God is sovereignly in control over all persecution.
- We are to entrust our lives to the faithful Creator.
- The biblical principle is suffering now but unimaginable, heavenly glory to follow.
- Rejoice in suffering for the gospel.
- Do not be frightened by the opposition.
- Practice patience, endurance, and faith.
- Be bold and never ashamed of the gospel.
- Defending one's self or appealing to legal and government protection is acceptable.
- Persevere in suffering for the gospel by God's enabling power and protection.
- God will punish those who afflict his people.
- Jesus has promised that his Church will prevail.

What We Can Do

At this very moment, in many places imprisoned Christians are being treated inhumanely for their faith. What are we to do? The Scripture is perfectly clear—we are to identify with them as if we were in prison beside them, remembering that we are all members of the one body of Christ:

> Remember those who are in prison, *as though in prison with them*, and those who are mistreated, since you also are in the body. (Heb. 13:3)

> For *you had compassion on those in prison*, and you joyfully accepted the plundering of your property, since you knew that

you yourselves had a better possession and an abiding one. (Heb. 10:34)

Then the King will say to those on his right, "Come, you who are blessed by my Father, inherit the kingdom prepared for you from the foundation of the world. . . . *I was in prison and you came to me.*" Then the righteous will answer him, saying, "Lord . . . when did we see you sick or in prison and visit you?" And the King will answer them, "Truly, I say to you, as you did it to one of the least of these my brothers, you did it to me." (Matt. 25:34–40)

As shepherd leaders, keep your congregation informed about the worldwide persecution of our brothers and sisters in Christ. Good organizations are providing up-to-date information about the worldwide persecution of believers. Have this material available for your local church. For current, accurate statistics, see the "World Watch List: The 50 Countries Where It's Most Dangerous to Follow Jesus" by Open Doors USA.

Prayer: Paul did not hesitate to ask for prayer that he might "be delivered from wicked and evil men" (2 Thess. 3:2). Prayer is one way of having "compassion on those in prison." You can "remember those who are in prison, as though in prison with them" by regularly praying for them.

Of course, you can pray generally for all Christians imprisoned throughout the world. But it would be much more relevant to you and your church if you pick a few countries or specific Christian leaders by name and focus on praying for them and their needs by name (see Eph. 6:19–20). Personally, I pray for those in Cuba, Russia, Iran, and North Korea who are being persecuted for the gospel.

Recently, a veteran missionary asked me to pray for a 21-year-old woman, a new convert who had been arrested for her faith and sent to a dungeon-like prison. What an encouragement to her and the missionary if thousands of Christians worldwide participated in an outflowing of prayer! This could sustain her in prison or even help with her release.

Other Ways to Minister:

- Donate financially to organizations that are helping suffering Christians worldwide.
- Get involved in distributing printed Bibles, or Christian books and Bibles in digital formats to believers in closed countries. More and more countries have outlawed such literature. Modern technology and the internet are providing new tools.
- Letters, email, or phone calls greatly encourage suffering believers and those who serve Christ in these hard places.
- Dedicate a bulletin board in your church building to provide up-to-date information on persecuted believers so your local body can pray.

Conclusion

Whether it is emotional tears or physical persecution, both are forms of suffering for Christ. And both have their God-given rewards: "For I consider that *the sufferings of this present time are not worth comparing with the glory that is to be revealed to us*" (Rom. 8:18). "For this light momentary affliction is preparing for us an eternal weight of glory beyond all comparison" (2 Cor. 4:17).

As leaders among the Lord's people, we should consider it a true honor to suffer for the sake of the Savior who suffered so much for us to secure our eternal salvation. Indeed: "Consider him who endured from sinners such hostility against himself, so that you may not grow weary or fainthearted" (Heb. 12:3).

Paul's example of serving the Lord Jesus with tears and facing organized persecution for the gospel should have inspired the Ephesian elders to persevere in serving the Lord and his people in the spiritually dark and hostile city of Ephesus. His example should encourage and strengthen us also.

KEY POINTS TO REMEMBER:

1. If you love people and are attentive to their needs, there will be times when you will weep over the many heartaches, conflicts, and hardships they face.

2. If the world hated and rejected Christ, it will hate and reject you as well. Be prepared!

3. To prepare yourself and the local church for suffering persecution *know* and *teach* what the Scriptures say about suffering for Christ.

4. Your theology, and especially your eschatology (the doctrine of last things), will determine your attitude and responses to persecution.

5. Lead the congregation in prayer for persecuted brothers and sisters around the world.

---

[1] *Encarta World English Dictionary*, 586.

[2] A phrase used often by Gordon D. Fee in *God's Empowering Presence: The Holy Spirit in the Letters of Paul* (Peabody, MA: Hendrickson, 1994).

[3] Jonathan Edwards, "*Men Naturally Are God's Enemies*," in *Works of Jonathan Edwards*, ed. Edward Hickman (Edinburgh: Banner of Truth, 1974), 2:132.

[4] Acts 9:16; 1 Cor. 4:9–13; 2 Cor. 4:8–12; 6:4–10; 11:22–29; 12:10.

[5] Alister McGrath, *C. S. Lewis: A Life* (Carol Stream, IL: Tyndale, 2013), 242–47 (esp. 244); Humphrey Carpenter, *The Inklings* (Boston: Houghton Mifflin, 1979), 228–230 (esp. 229).

[6] John Stott, *The Gospel & The End of Time: The Message of 1 & 2 Thessalonians* (Downers Grove, IL: InterVarsity, 1991), 65.

[7] Gordon Fee, *Paul's Letter to the Philippians*, NICNT (Grand Rapids: Eerdmans, 1995), 170–171.

CHAPTER 4

Remember My Teaching and Evangelistic Ministries

You yourselves know . . . how I did not shrink from declaring to you anything that was profitable, and teaching you in public and from house to house, testifying both to Jews and to Greeks of repentance toward God and of faith in our Lord Jesus Christ.

(Acts 20:18b, 20–21)

Paul began his pastoral charge by calling the elders to remember how he lived among them for three years—serving the Lord with all humility and heartbreaking tears, and facing hostile, organized persecution. Next, he reminded them of how he taught them and witnessed publicly of Christ to all people.

Like Jesus, in whose steps he closely followed, Paul was a consummate teacher, educator, and herald of the gospel. Here in verse 20, Paul essentially indicates that he did his work of teaching and evangelism *in the most thorough way*. As Paul leaves, it is now for the Ephesian elders to carry on with the work that he started. They also must be thorough in their teaching ministry.

This is a very important section of Paul's address. In verse 27 he repeats (with slight variation) what he states here in verse 20: "I did not shrink from declaring to you anything that was profitable."

HOLDING BACK NOTHING THAT WAS PROFITABLE

Do not miss the significance of this claim: "I did not shrink from declaring to you anything that was profitable." *There was no aspect of Christian doctrine that Paul neglected to teach. He did not omit some of the finer details of the faith, nor adapt the truth to the spirit of the age.*

The story is told of some seventeenth-century missionaries to China who compromised the biblical message of sin and the cross in order not to cause offense to their hearers, but in the end betrayed the biblical gospel and Jesus Christ. Of this incident, "Professor Hugh Trevor-Roper has written, 'we do not learn that they made many lasting converts by the unobjectionable residue of the story.'"[1]

> The Ephesian elders lacked nothing in their theological education for teaching the gospel or living lives pleasing to God.

Some preachers avoid speaking of certain doctrines that might be offensive or hard to understand. Paul resisted this temptation. All that Christ taught him, he had taught the Ephesian elders. As a result, these elders lacked nothing in their theological education for teaching the gospel or living lives pleasing to God.

Declaring All that Is Profitable

There was not one single point of doctrine that was "profitable" (i.e., "helpful," "beneficial") to the elders that Paul held back from them. He was emphatic about this matter: "I did not shrink from declaring to you anything that was profitable."

The term "declaring" carries the ideas of providing information and publicly proclaiming and teaching it.[2] What he declared, Paul later described as "the whole counsel of God" (v. 27). *To prepare and strengthen the elders for their shepherding task they needed to know "the whole counsel of God." This Paul faithfully declared to them. His teaching ministry was thorough and in-depth.*

The elders could trust Paul precisely because he held back no information that was beneficial to their knowledge of God, Christ, and the gospel. He didn't just teach a few pet subjects. The elders were not going to be surprised after he departed to learn hidden truths he had concealed. They knew all that they needed in order to teach, lead, and protect the church.

Holding Back the Full Truth

Tragically, there are churches that do shrink from declaring the whole counsel of God. They are afraid that what the Bible says will turn people away from the church. They assume that people don't want to hear Bible doctrine or the exposition of God's Word.

Too many Christians are being fed simplistic sermonettes to keep them happy and coming back to church. Of this kind of teaching it is often said to be "a mile wide and a half-inch deep." Or more humorously, "Sermonettes make Christianettes." As a result of weak, shallow teaching, the people remain Christian infants throughout their whole lives. They know little of God's holy Book. They have never been taught Romans, Galatians, Ephesians, or Hebrews. They are ill-informed about justification by faith, propitiation by the blood of Christ, redemption, reconciliation through the Cross, adoption, union with Christ, sanctification, or the indwelling presence of the Holy Spirit.

As a result, the people do not grow "in the grace and knowledge of our Lord and Savior Jesus Christ" (2 Peter 3:18). They are not being properly equipped for their "work of ministry" (Eph. 4:11–12).

But who is at fault and responsible for this situation? In large part, it is the disobedient shepherds who do not feed the sheep all that is "profitable" from God's Word for their spiritual health and growth. So we can ask, just as the prophet Ezekiel asked of Israel's leaders, "should not shepherds feed the sheep?" (Ezek. 34:2).

From his must-read book, *The Gathering Storm: Secularism, Culture, and the Church*, R. Albert Mohler makes this significant comment:

> The secular age exerts a subtle but constant influence on churches and Christians. If not careful, churches will look less and less like churches and more and more like the secular world around them. In a sense, liberal theology begins to slowly replace orthodox faith. Or, in other cases, churches simply stop talking about or teaching important truths revealed in the Bible. . . . The failure to teach truth eventually leads to failure of Christ's people even to know the truth.[3]

Be Prepared to Teach the Whole Counsel of God

What Paul reveals about his way of teaching *must now become our strategy of education*: Teach the whole counsel of God! Teach the whole of Scripture. Teach all the doctrines of Scripture. *Do not hold back anything that is profitable for the people's growth in Christlikeness.* Do not fear or steer clear of those aspects of Christian doctrine that are offensive to Western secular society.

Secularists are not afraid to propagate their godless, humanistic philosophies. They are quite bold. Why then should we be afraid to teach the whole plan of God, the greatest message ever told, the message that offers eternal life? Secularists hold out no such messages, no such hope.

As an eldership team, take seriously the matter of teaching the whole counsel of God and holding back nothing of profit for the people. Have a clear plan for teaching the whole message of Scripture to all the people under your pastoral care. In this way you will prove yourselves to be faithful shepherds feeding God's flock on God's food.

Helpful Resources: Many excellent resources are available today in book and digital form for educating your people in the whole of Scripture and in systematic Bible doctrine.

Biblical elders are to be actively engaged
in Christian education.

Have these resources available, and encourage your people to use them in group or private study. *Don't be passive about educating your people in Scripture and Bible doctrine.* Biblical elders are to be actively engaged in Christian education.

On my visit to a certain church I noticed over the entry doors to the main auditorium in large gold letters, "For the Equipping of the Saints," a quote from Ephesians 4:12. Seeing these words boldly displayed led me to conclude: *The elders of this church are real biblical elders who take seriously the responsibility of feeding the flock a healthy diet of God-breathed words.* "All Scripture is breathed out by God and profitable for teaching" (2 Tim. 3:16).

These elders knew what they were doing. Through the preaching of the Word of God by Spirit-gifted teachers, they were preparing God's people to do "the work of ministry" that God had gifted them to do in order to build up the body of Christ (Eph. 4:12).

At another church I visited, the elders of the church explained to me that they train all their elders to be theologians—students of God and the Bible. They take seriously the biblical qualification that a Christian elder must be "able to give instruction in sound doctrine" and be able also "to rebuke those who contradict" sound biblical teaching (Titus 1:9). This takes deliberate, planned training on the part of the church leadership.

Tragically, in too many churches, the people called elders are untrained in Bible doctrine, ignorant of divine Scripture, and biblically unqualified to serve.

"And I will give you shepherds after my own heart,
who will feed you with knowledge and understanding."
Jeremiah 3:15

May it never be that the Lord must say of us, as he said to the Old Testament priests in Hosea's day, "My people are destroyed for lack of knowledge" (Hos. 4:6). Instead, may we be the kind of shepherds the Lord promised to give his people: "And I will give you shepherds after my own heart, who will feed you with knowledge and understanding" (Jer. 3:15).

TEACHING BOTH IN PUBLIC AND IN PRIVATE

To further emphasize the thoroughness of his teaching ministry, Paul reminded his fellow workers that he taught them publicly and privately: "teaching you in public and from house to house." By the term "teaching,"[4] Paul meant he "provided a structured explanation of the gospel, with the goal that the Ephesians would remember the content of the teaching."[5]

Teaching in Public

Paul's ministry was characterized by open public teaching that anyone could hear and understand and believe. When he was in the city of Ephesus, Paul taught publicly in the synagogue and "in the hall of Tyrannus" (Acts 19:9).

Paul did not create a secret society. He did not teach a hidden, esoteric message for only a few initiated people to understand. As a Christian teacher, he toiled and struggled to "present everyone mature in Christ":[6]

> Him [Christ] we proclaim, warning everyone and teaching everyone with all wisdom, that we may present everyone mature in Christ. For this I toil, struggling with all his energy that he powerfully works within me. (Col. 1:28–29)

The gospel message he proclaimed was a universal message for all people to hear and believe. Openness and transparency marked his presentation of his God-given message.

Teaching in Homes

Not only did Paul teach publicly, he taught "from house to house," in more private, intimate meetings. Teaching in homes was an effective and natural way of spreading the gospel.

A home provides an informal, relaxed atmosphere for teaching the Bible, for interaction with the teacher, and for building personal relationships between student and teacher. The home provides a comfortable atmosphere for family members, friends, neighbors, and relatives to meet together and be taught.

For me some of my most enjoyable, rewarding times of teaching have been in my home. Recently a friend reminded me of our two-year study of the book of Acts in my home every Wednesday night. He said it was an unforgettable time in his life, as well as life changing.

> For the elder not Spirit-gifted at speaking to a large or mixed audience, the home is the ideal place to teach the Scriptures and disciple believers.

In the home environment people can ask questions directly. This allows people to get to know you as a person, not just as a teacher in front of an audience. In a home environment food and snacks can be served, which helps people to relax and enjoy themselves. It creates warmth and friendship and breaks down barriers. *The home is the perfect setting for in-depth teaching of the whole counsel of God.* And for the elder not Spirit-gifted at speaking to a large or mixed audience, the home is the ideal place to teach the Scriptures and disciple believers.

A Creative Teacher: Paul used every means at his disposal to spread the gospel message. He was a creative, flexible teacher and a bold proclaimer of the gospel. *We should follow Paul's example and be resourceful, thorough, and forthright in our dissemination of the greatest story ever given us to tell.*

"If there is a religion in the world which exalts
the office of teaching, it is safe to say that
it is the religion of Jesus Christ." —James Orr

A PREACHING-TEACHING MOVEMENT

Throughout the New Testament, extraordinary emphasis is placed on the centrality of teaching God's message, the gospel. From the very beginning, Christianity was a preaching-teaching movement:

- Jesus came preaching the good news of the kingdom of God. Jesus was predominantly a teacher.
- Jesus charged his disciples with the Great Commission, which includes "teaching [new disciples] to observe all that I have commanded you" (Matt. 28:20).
- The book of Acts records the Great Commission in action— the proclamation of the gospel and instruction of new believers.
- The earliest Christians steadfastly "devoted themselves to the apostles' teaching" (Acts 2:42).
- In Acts, "the apostles' ministry of preaching and teaching is mentioned more often than any other activity in which they were engaged."[7]
- Acts 6:4 best summarizes the apostles' priorities: "We will devote ourselves to prayer and to the ministry of the word."
- Paul dedicated his life to teaching the doctrines of Christ and to helping God's people grow "in the knowledge of God" (Col. 1:10).
- God commissioned Paul uniquely as his steward "to make the word of God fully known" (Col. 1:25).
- To his close associate, Timothy, Paul wrote: "I charge you in the presence of God and of Christ Jesus, who is to judge the living and the dead, and by his appearing and his king-

dom: preach the word; be ready in season and out of season; reprove, rebuke, and exhort, with complete patience and teaching" (2 Tim. 4:1–2); "What you have heard from me in the presence of many witnesses entrust to faithful men who will be able to teach others also" (2 Tim. 2:2).

"Teaching was a mark of Pauline churches," states I. Howard Marshall.[8] James Orr, best known as general editor of the multi-volume *International Standard Bible Encyclopedia*, comments on the preeminence of teaching in the early Christian communities: "If there is a religion in the world which exalts the office of teaching, it is safe to say that it is the religion of Jesus Christ."[9]

A Word-Centered Ministry

In Acts 20:20–21, Paul uses three different Greek terms to describe and explain oral communication of information: "declaring,"[10] "teaching,"[11] and "testifying."[12] Similar terms used throughout the discourse are "proclaim,"[13] "testify,"[14] and "admonish."[15]

Paul had been entrusted with an authoritative and urgent message from God to be proclaimed and taught to all people. His ministry was a Word-centered ministry, delivering God's message of "the way of salvation." In fact, Paul calls himself a "herald"[16] appointed to announce publicly to all people God's good news of sins forgiven and eternal life through the crucified, risen Messiah.

There is no more important and urgent message on this earth than God's promise of eternal life: "And this is the promise that he made to us—eternal life" (1 John 2:25).

Paul had been entrusted with an authoritative and urgent message from God to be proclaimed and taught to all people. His ministry was a Word-centered ministry.

An Elder Requirement: It makes sense then, why Paul requires that a biblical elder "must hold firm to the trustworthy word [the gospel] as taught [by the apostles]" (Titus 1:9). Moreover, an elder must "be able to give instruction in sound doctrine and also to rebuke those who contradict it" (Titus 1:9). *A biblical elder must know sound doctrine, be able to give instruction in sound doctrine, and be able to defend sound doctrine.* Otherwise a person is dangerously unfit and unqualified to serve God's people as a shepherd elder.

The Desperate Need for Bible Teaching: From Africa a friend wrote of the need for more serious Bible teaching:

> So much of the [problems within the churches] is a neglect of the Bible. Most of these denominations teach their pet doctrines, and don't teach the Bible. . . . The need for believers is to read and study and teach the Bibles *they already have.* There is a phenomenal lack of basic biblical knowledge. . . . [Instead, they have] lots of emotion and lots of merit-based salvation thinking. My contacts here tell me it is very rare for pastors to actually study the Bible or teach from the Bible. Usually just sermons on tithing, ad nauseum.

What this friend reports of the problem in some African churches can be observed in many other places in the world. There is a crying need for a fresh "back to the Bible" movement. This would mean a renewed confidence in the divine origin of Scripture, the authority of Scripture, the sufficiency of Scripture, and the preaching of Scripture. And, I must add, a love by the people for hearing the Scriptures preached with Spirit-gifted authority.

BEARING WITNESS TO BOTH JEWS AND GENTILES

Paul also wanted the Ephesian elders to remember how he testified to both Jews and to Greeks—two hostile, estranged groups that despised each other. The word "testifying" is a strong term meaning "to make a solemn declaration about the truth of something, testify of, bear witness to (originally under oath)."[17] The term can also carry the idea of "[exhorting] with authority in matters of extraordinary importance."[18]

Paul was steadfast in presenting the universal message of salvation for both Jews and Gentiles: "For there is no distinction between Jew and Greek; for the same Lord is Lord of all, bestowing his riches on *all who call on him*" (Rom. 10:12).

Repentance and Faith

Paul's message to both Jews and Gentiles was the same—"repentance toward God" and "faith in our Lord Jesus Christ" (v. 21).[19] This is a brief summary statement of his gospel message viewed from "its final appeal."[20] There is a lot packed into these few words. Paul's message was a serious message about "repentance," "faith," "God," and the "Lord Jesus Christ."

The gospel call requires a response. The proper response is "repentance toward God." Why repentance toward God? That is because fallen humanity has grievously sinned against God the Creator by their worship of man-made idols and gross sexual immorality (see Rom. 1:18–32). They have rejected and spurned their Creator and rightly deserve divine judgment. Thus the need for sincere "repentance toward God."[21] D. A. Carson's definition of repentance bears repeating:

> What this means is not a merely intellectual change of mind or mere grief, still less doing penance, but a radical transformation of the entire person, a fundamental turnaround involving mind and action and including overtones of grief, which results in "fruit in keeping with repentance." Of course, all this assumes that man's actions are fundamentally off course and need radical change.[22]

The proper response also includes "faith in our Lord Jesus Christ," who is Lord of all creation and the only true Savior of lost mankind. By believing in the Lord Jesus Christ, his unique person and work on the cross for sinners, a person can be forgiven of all sin, saved from God's wrath, and be born again by the Holy Spirit.

Of the two terms regarding conversion, *faith* is clearly the predominate word that permeates Paul's letters:

> That I may . . . be found in him, not having a righteousness of my own that comes from the law, but that which comes through faith in Christ, the righteousness from God that depends on faith. (Phil. 3:8–9)

> If you confess with your mouth that Jesus is Lord and believe in your heart that God raised him from the dead, you will be saved. For with the heart one believes and is justified, and with the mouth one confesses and is saved. (Rom. 10:9–10)

Neither repentance nor faith, however, are the basis for salvation. The basis or ground of our salvation is the sacrificial death of Christ upon the cross. It is the object of faith—the crucified, risen Lord Jesus Christ—that saves the sinner. Faith and repentance are the instrumental means through which sinners are converted.

A Message from Christ: Paul received the message "of repentance toward God and of faith in our Lord Jesus Christ" directly from the risen, exalted Lord Jesus Christ. He did not invent this message out of his own clever mind. Steven Lawson reminds us that,

> The Gospel has not been crafted by any church, drafted by any denomination, nor scripted by any seminary. No pastor or leaders have concocted it. Instead, the Gospel has come down in purest form from the highest courts of Heaven, and from the infinite genius of God.[23]

This message must now be protected and propagated by the entire believing community, led by its pastoral elders.

Evangelize or Fossilize

All believers have a message from God to declare to the world "the message of reconciliation" (2 Cor. 5:19). We are "ambassadors for Christ" (2 Cor. 5:20). To the first Christians in the pagan city of Colossae, Paul appeals to them to be always prepared to witness to unbelievers:

> Walk in wisdom toward outsiders [unbelievers], making the best use of the time [opportunities]. Let your speech always be gracious, seasoned with salt, so that you may know how you ought to answer each person. (Col. 4:5–6)

So instructs the apostle Peter: "Always being prepared to make a defense to anyone who asks you for a reason for the hope that is in you; yet do it with gentleness and respect" (1 Peter 3:15).

As gospel leaders, you need to model a love for the lost and an ability to explain God's way of salvation through Christ graciously and tactfully. To have God's heartbeat, you need to have a heart for evangelism and for the lost. The phrase "evangelize or fossilize" certainly rings true.[24] If a church is to grow, you need to tell people of repentance toward God and faith in our Lord Jesus Christ.

KEY POINTS TO REMEMBER

1. Teach the whole of Scripture; teach all the doctrines of Scripture; do not hold back anything that is beneficial for the growth and protection of your people.

2. Biblical elders are in the education and communication business. We have an urgent message from God about sins forgiven and eternal salvation.

3. A biblical elder must be able to give instruction in "sound doctrine" and be able to defend "sound doctrine" (Titus 1:9).

4. Be prepared to preach "repentance toward God" and "faith in our Lord Jesus Christ."

5. As gospel leaders you need to model a love for witnessing to "the hope that is in you."

---

[1] John R. W. Stott, *Our Guilty Silence* (Chicago: InterVarsity, 1967), 45.

[2] BDAG, s.v. "ἀναγγελλω," 59, "to provide information, disclose, announce, proclaim, teach."

[3] R. Albert Mohler Jr., *The Gathering Storm: Secularism, Culture, and the Church* (Nashville, TN: Nelson Books, 2020), 22.

[4] BDAG, s.v. "διδασκω," 241, "to provide instruction in a formal or informal setting, teach."

[5] Eckhard J. Schnabel, *Acts*, ECNT (Grand Rapids: Zondervan, 2012), 840.

[6] Acts 11:26; 15:35; 18:11; 20:20; 28:31; 1 Cor. 4:17; Col. 1:28.

[7] Steven J. Lawson, *Famine in the Land: A Passionate Call for Expository Preaching* (Chicago: Moody, 2003), 31.

[8] I. Howard Marshall, *The Pastoral Epistles*, ICC (Edinburgh: T&T Clark, 1999), 435.

[9] James Orr, *The Christian View of God and the World* (Grand Rapids: Eerdmans, 1948), 20.

[10] BDAG, s.v. "ἀναγγελλω," 59, "to provide information, disclose, announce, proclaim, teach." Also used in Acts 20:27.

[11] διδασκω [*didaskō*]. See endnote 5 and Schnabel's definition given in the text.

[12] διαμαρτυρομαι [*diamartyromai*]. Also used in verse 24.

[13] BDAG, s.v. "κηρυσσω," 543, "the verb frequently designates the oral proclamation of the gospel of Jesus Christ." Used in Acts 20:25.

[14] BDAG, s.v. "μαρτυρομαι," 619, "to affirm something with solemnity, testify, bear witness." Used in Acts 20:26.

[15] νουθετεω [*noutheteō*]. Used also in Acts 20:31.

[16] κῆρυξ [*kēryx*], 1 Tim. 2:7; 2 Tim. 1:11; also a "preacher," "proclaimer," καταγγελευς [*katangeleus*] in Acts 17:18.

[17] BDAG, s.v. "διαμαρτυρομαι," 233.

[18] BDAG, s.v. "διαμαρτυρομαι," 233.

[19] "The two elements in conversion, repentance and faith, are introduced by one article (την [*tēn*]), which has the effect of binding them closely together" (C. K. Barrett, *The Acts of the Apostles*, vol. 2, ICC [Edinburgh: T&T Clark, 1998], 969).

[20] David G. Peterson, *Acts of the Apostles*, PNTC (Grand Rapids: Eerdmans, 2009), 565.

[21] See the verb form (μετανοεω) Matt. 11:21; 12:41; Mark 1:4, 15; 6:12; Luke 13:3, 5; 15:7; Acts 3:19; 19:4; 26:20; Rev. 16:9. See the noun form (μετανοια) Matt. 3:8; Luke 3:8; 5:32; 24:47; Acts 5:31; 11:18; Rom. 2:4; 2 Peter 3:9.

[22] D. A. Carson, *Matthew 1–12*, EBC (Grand Rapids: Zondervan, 1995), 99.

[23] Quote by Steven J. Lawson in an unpublished sermon on Romans 1:1. Used by permission.

[24] Herbert Lockyer, *Evangelize or Fossilize: The Urgent Mission of the Church* (New Kensington, PA: Whitaker House, 1938, repr. 2014).

CHAPTER 5

Total Dedication to Christ and the Gospel of the Grace of God

And now, behold, I am going to Jerusalem, constrained by the Spirit, not knowing what will happen to me there, except that the Holy Spirit testifies to me in every city that imprisonment and afflictions await me. But I do not account my life of any value nor as precious to myself, if only I may finish my course and the ministry that I received from the Lord Jesus, to testify to the gospel of the grace of God.
(Acts 20:22–24)

Paul now shifts gears from reminding the elders of his past record of serving the Lord in Ephesus to informing them of his present travel plans: "And now, behold, I am going to Jerusalem." In this section of his address, Paul's courage, total dedication to Christ, and faithfulness in gospel witness stand out as further characteristics of a life to be emulated.

A REMARKABLE EXAMPLE OF COURAGE

As previously noted, Paul's meeting with the Ephesian elders occurred while on his journey east to Jerusalem. He was hoping to arrive for the Feast of Pentecost in the spring of AD 57. He was not traveling alone. With him were representatives from a number of Gentile churches whose purpose was to deliver a financial contribution they had collected to help the poverty-stricken Christians in Jerusalem.

Paul had put a great deal of effort into this enterprise, including the arduous journey back to Jerusalem. Prophetic predictions of "imprisonment and afflictions" occurring in Jerusalem (v. 23) were not going to deter him. *He was a man of outstanding courage*, not easily deterred by opposition or suffering.

The Spirit's Warnings of Persecution

As he and his traveling companions continued on their way east, the Holy Spirit repeatedly spoke to Paul through prophets "that imprisonment [bonds] and afflictions await[ed]" him. There would thus be no surprises ahead, no unforeseen tragedies, no blind fate, or unexplainable accidents. He knew exactly what to expect! Yet he still marched on.

The Leading of the Spirit: In Acts we see the constant leading of the Holy Spirit in advancing the gospel message outward from Jerusalem "to the end of the earth" (Acts 1:8). Paul was sensitive to the Holy Spirit's voice and direction. *He would want the elders also to be always sensitive to the leading and empowering presence of the Spirit in their lives.* In verse 28 Paul reminded the elders that it was the Holy Spirit himself who placed them in the church as overseers to shepherd God's flock.

In light of the Spirit's repeated warnings of suffering and persecution, Paul could have taken this opportunity to turn back or to leave gospel ministry altogether. He could claim that the Holy Spirit did not want him to go to Jerusalem. But the Holy Spirit did not forbid him from going to Jerusalem, nor did the Spirit predict death. The Spirit predicted the dangers Paul would face in Jerusalem, preparing him for the inevitable events that lay ahead.

Despite these ominous warnings of suffering, Paul was convinced that it was the right thing for him to go to Jerusalem.

A REMARKABLE EXAMPLE OF TOTAL COMMITMENT TO FINISHING HIS ASSIGNED TASK

The Holy Spirit's warnings of "imprisonment and afflictions" provide the context for Paul's next statement, which gives us a remarkable insight into his way of thinking and personal motivation:

> But I do not account my life of any value nor as precious to myself, if only I may finish my course and the ministry that I received from the Lord Jesus, to testify to the gospel of the grace of God. (Acts 20:24)

Here is one of the most challenging testimonies of personal devotion to Christ recorded in the New Testament. Nothing mattered more to Paul than faithfully completing the task given to him by his Lord, "to testify to the gospel of the grace of God."

The elders needed now, in his absence, to be faithful to their Spirit-assigned task to shepherd the church of God (v. 28). And so do you!

Assessing the Value of His Life

Paul states: "But I do not account my life of any value nor as precious to myself." What is most precious and most valuable to any of us? Is it not life, our conscious existence here on this earth? Yet Paul was willing to lose his life for the sake of finishing both the course God had set before him, and the ministry that he received directly from the Lord Jesus.

Here is a man who clearly understood his God-given priorities. He was willing to lose his life to gain his life. He denied himself, took up his cross, and followed Jesus (Mark 8:34–37).

Paul saw that the need to finish his God-appointed gospel mission far outweighed the value of his own life. He was so dedicated to Christ and the gospel that his own future, reputation, comfort, and security were of little account. He compared knowing and serving Christ to any other of his life's achievements:

> But whatever gain I had, I counted as loss for the sake of Christ. Indeed, I count everything as loss because of the surpassing worth of knowing Christ Jesus my Lord. For his sake I have suffered the loss of all things and count them as rubbish, in order that I may gain Christ. (Phil. 3:7–8)

We see here the theme of self-sacrifice for Christ and the gospel, which runs through the entire speech.

A Course to Be Finished

Paul used an athletic metaphor to illustrate his thinking. He viewed himself as a runner who must finish the course set before him by the Lord. This course is a marathon, a cross-country race; it is not a sprint or a dash. It is a lifelong race.

In a cross-country race there are unexpected ups and downs, and obstacles like streams to cross and rocks in the path. Life is similar, with hills and sudden valleys, easy times and hard, serious impediments, sudden sunshine, unforeseen storms. No matter. The runner must persevere, continue, and finish the course.

Paul was intent on finishing the course God had designed for him, despite its many dangers and adversities. While in prison in Rome facing impending death, he confidently wrote Timothy that he had finished his course:

> For I am already being poured out as a drink offering, and
> the time of my departure has come. I have fought the good
> fight, I have finished the race [course], I have kept the faith.
> (2 Tim. 4:6–7)

My challenge to you, my dear reader, is that you make it your
personal life goal to be able to say at the end of life, "I have finished
the race, I have kept the faith." This noble goal is for all exempla-
ry church leaders: "Let us run with endurance the race that is set
before us" (Heb. 12:1).

> Make it your personal life goal to be able to say
> at the end of life, "I have finished the race,
> I have kept the faith."

A Ministry to Be Completed

Not only did Paul have a course to finish, he had a "ministry" to complete. This "ministry" (διακονια [*diakonia*]) was given to him directly
by the risen Lord: "I received [it] from the Lord Jesus to testify to
the gospel of the grace of God" (v. 24). The fact that he received this
commission directly from the Lord Jesus himself made its fulfillment
all the more urgent—so urgent that it was more important to Paul
than his very own life.

Jesus Is Lord: Paul's total devotion to the Lord Jesus Christ was based
firmly on his belief in Jesus's divine nature and sacrificial atoning
work for sinners. Jesus is both Creator and Redeemer, and thus he
must be wholeheartedly worshipped and served:

- "For in him the whole fullness of deity dwells bodily."
  (Col. 2:9; also Rom. 9:5; Titus 2:13)
- "He is the image of the invisible God, the firstborn of all
  creation. For by him all things were created." (Col. 1:15–16)

- "For our sake he made him [Jesus] to be sin who knew no sin, so that in him we might become the righteousness of God." (2 Cor. 5:21)
- "[All are] justified by his grace as a gift, through the redemption that is in Christ Jesus, whom God put forward as a propitiation by his blood." (Rom. 3:24–25)
- "For what we proclaim is not ourselves, but Jesus Christ as Lord." (2 Cor. 4:5)
- "At the name of Jesus every knee should bow, in heaven and on earth and under the earth, and every tongue confess that Jesus Christ is Lord, to the glory of God the Father." (Phil. 2:10–11)

C. T. (Charles Thomas) Studd, pioneer missionary to China, India, and Africa, understood Paul's reasoning and responded by declaring: "If Jesus Christ be God and died for me, then no sacrifice can be too great for me to make for Him."[1] Similarly, Isaac Watts's famous hymn, "When I Survey the Wonderous Cross," concludes with the words: "Love so amazing, so divine, demands my soul, my life, my all." Paul would have agreed with Watts's and Studd's impeccable logic. Indeed, his logic was the same:

For the love of Christ controls us, because we have concluded this: that one has died for all, therefore all have died; and he died for all, that those who live might no longer live for themselves but for him who for their sake died and was raised. (2 Cor. 5:14–15)

"Whatever else the Christian faith is," concludes biblical commentator Gordon Fee, "and whatever Christian life is all about, it finds its central focus ever and always on Christ."[2]

"If Jesus Christ be God and died for me, then
no sacrifice can be too great for me to make
for Him."—C. T. Studd

Eric Alexander is considered by many to be one of the outstanding preachers of our time. Now retired, he served a church in Glasgow, Scotland, for years. Eric was led to faith in Christ by his older brother, a devout Christian man who had served three years in full-time Christian ministry, and who died at the age of only twenty-nine. After his death, Eric was given his brother's personal journal where he found these moving words:

> In some people's lives, Jesus Christ has no place. In every Christian's life, Jesus Christ does have a place. In many Christians' lives, Jesus Christ has a prominent place. But in a few Christians' lives, I have found that Jesus Christ has a pre-eminent place.[3]

What place does Jesus Christ have in your life?

A REMARKABLE EXAMPLE OF TESTIFYING TO THE GOSPEL OF THE GRACE OF GOD

Paul was under divine marching orders "to testify"[4] to the gospel of God's grace. "For if I preach the gospel, that gives me no ground for boasting. For necessity is laid upon me. Woe to me if I do not preach the gospel" (1 Cor. 9:16).

The *Euangelion*

The word "gospel" means "good news," "glad tidings" (εὐαγγελιον [*euangelion*]).[5] One writer asks, "Could it be that the biblical gospel is in fact the very *best* news imaginable?"[6] I say, "Yes!"

The "best news imaginable" is about forgiveness of sins, reconciliation with God, adoption into God's family, and deliverance from spiritual darkness, wrath, and death. The gospel includes the indwelling presence of the Holy Spirit and the exhilarating promise of eternal life and a new heaven and earth. Paul succinctly summarized it as "the word of truth, the gospel of your salvation" (Eph. 1:13).

This good news is made possible only by the grace of God displayed in the incarnation of the Son of God, his perfect life, his substitutionary death upon the cross, and his victorious bodily resurrection from the dead. Paul's whole life was set apart for the public proclamation of the good news of the grace of God.[7] This was his primary ministry in life, to be a servant of the gospel (Col. 1:23).

The Grace of God

The gospel is described in verse 24 as "the gospel of the grace of God."[8] Grace is one of the most prominent words of the Christian faith and a major pillar of Paul's gospel. God's grace is his divine favor, freely given to the undeserving, which cannot be earned or merited.

The doctrine of God's undeserved and unmerited grace to us is one of the famous five *solas* of the sixteenth century Reformation: *sola Scriptura* (Scripture alone), *sola gratia* (grace alone), *sola fide* (faith alone), *solus Christus* (Christ alone), and *soli Deo gloria* (glory to God alone). Divine grace is foundational to understanding the biblical gospel message. Gordon Fee puts it so eloquently:

> Grace is the beginning and the end of the Christian gospel; it is the single word that most fully expresses what God has done and will do for his people in Christ Jesus; nothing is deserved, everything is freely given.[9]

74

Understanding Sin and Wrath: You cannot understand the good news of the grace of God if you don't first understand the bad news. The bad news is the horrible nature of sin, mankind's stubborn rebellion against the Creator, and God's just wrath against our lawlessness, disobedience of his law, and rejection of his divine authority. See how Paul places saving grace in the context of mankind's spiritual deadness and sin:

> And *you were dead in the trespasses and sins* in which you once walked, following the course of this world, following the prince of the power of the air, the spirit that is now at work in the sons of disobedience—among whom we all once lived in the passions of our flesh, carrying out the desires of the body and the mind, and were by nature children of wrath, like the rest of mankind. But God, being rich in mercy, because of the great love with which he loved us, even when we were dead in our trespasses, made us alive together with Christ—by grace you have been saved. (Eph. 2:1–5)

Understand that God does not owe us anything but righteous judgment. His grace to us is not because we deserve it, or because we are such nice people that he can't help but love us. God's grace is his kind and extravagant initiative to provide for the "ungodly" a means of salvation we could never achieve on our own, no matter how hard we try. Salvation is all of his grace from beginning to end—in fact, "grace is what enables sinners to believe (Acts 18:27)."[10]

"Amazing Grace, How Sweet the Sound"

God's lavish grace dominated Paul's thinking and teaching. In his letters he loved magnifying God's matchless, free grace to undeserving sinners:

> to the praise of his glorious grace, with which he has blessed [freely given] us in the Beloved. In him we have redemption through his blood, the forgiveness of our trespasses, *accord-*

ing to the riches of his grace, which he lavished upon us, in all wisdom and insight making known to us the mystery of his will, according to his purpose, which he set forth in Christ. (Eph. 1:6–9)

Paul makes clear that the redemption and forgiveness God provides is not "out of," but "according to the riches of his grace, which he lavished upon us" (Eph. 1:7–8).

Suppose you were to ask a very wealthy man for his support for a worthy cause. After listening to your presentation, he says, "Well, I think I would like to help you out." He then takes out his wallet and hands you a $20 bill. Perhaps you expected him to offer you $10,000 or so. He has given you *out of* his riches, not *according to* his riches. However, if he offered you a book of signed blank checks and said, "Take these checks, and fill them out for whatever you need; there is no limit to what you may spend on this important cause." That offer would be *according to* his riches.[11]

Grace reveals the character of God. He is "the God of all grace" (1 Peter 5:10). This grace originated in the mind and heart of God out of his great love. God so loved the world that he *gave* his only Son to provide salvation for sinners.

The Great and Glorious Doctrine of the Grace of God: *In all the world, and among all religions, there is no other message of salvation like the gospel of God's grace to sinners provided by the substitutionary death and bodily resurrection of Jesus.* No wonder this grace naturally leads to deep, heartfelt praise and worship: "to the praise of his glorious grace, with which he has blessed us in the Beloved" (Eph. 1:6).

The message of the grace of God makes us want to sing of his grace. If you doubt this, look at all the many inspiring hymns that have been written about God's marvelous, matchless grace. In the unforgettable words of John Newton:

Amazing grace! How sweet the sound that saved a wretch like me! I once was lost but now am found; was blind, but now I see.

When we've been there ten thousand years, bright shining as the sun, We've no less days to sing God's praise than when we first begun.

No wonder Paul was so taken with the doctrine of the gospel of the grace of God. It moved him to be willing to give his life "to testify to the gospel of the grace of God." What is your response to the message of the grace of God?

BE PREPARED TO KNOW AND DEFEND THE GOSPEL OF THE GRACE OF GOD

Paul reminded the Ephesian elders that his life's work was to testify to the great and glorious gospel of the grace of God. And that he did faithfully! But now he was leaving; it was his final departure. Who would protect and further testify to the "the gospel of the grace of God"? Who would stop the false teachers who distort the gospel of the grace of God and cause division within the church? *This must be the responsibility of those the Holy Spirit placed as overseers to shepherd the church of God,* the elders of the church!

Opponents of the Grace of God Alone

We know from Acts and Paul's letter to the Galatians that one of the earliest major attacks on the gospel was the Judaizers' assault on the doctrine of the grace of God. To the churches of Galatia Paul wrote: "I am astonished that you are so quickly deserting him who called you in the grace of Christ and are turning to a different gospel" (Gal. 1:6).

Self-Salvation: Today, it is no different. People want a law-based, merit-based, self-salvation program. They take pride in their good deeds and religiosity, and believe they deserve God's favor. Someone told a friend of mine, "If anyone deserves to go to heaven, it is me." I read in a so-called Christian publication these words, "We are saved by grace, after all that we have done."

> Prepare yourself to know well and to defend well the biblical teaching on salvation by God's grace alone, through Christ alone, through faith alone.

Most people do not want to hear or face that they are lost sinners who need to depend totally on God's grace alone for their salvation. Therefore, prepare yourself to know well and to defend well the biblical teaching on salvation by God's grace alone, through Christ alone, through faith alone:

> All . . . are justified by his grace as a gift, through the redemption that is in Christ Jesus, whom God put forward as a propitiation by his blood, to be received by faith." (Rom. 3:23–25)

Protectors and Propagators of God's Grace

As God's shepherds of God's flock, *you are protectors and transmitters of the good news message of God's matchless grace.* This is why God requires that first and foremost a biblical elder "must hold firm to the trustworthy word [gospel] as taught [by Paul]" (Titus 1:9).

No one should ever be appointed as a church elder who is not able and willing to defend the truths of God's grace in salvation.

Search the Scriptures: In light of all that Paul and the other biblical writers say about God's amazing grace, you should study the subject more, think about it more, and sing about it more.

You should want your church to be grace-centered, gospel-centered, Bible-centered, Christ-centered, and mission-centered.

This will not happen if you don't understand the biblical teaching on grace, or if you are ashamed of the gospel of grace, or if you are unwilling to suffer for the sake of the gospel.

BE PREPARED TO SACRIFICE YOUR LIFE FOR CHRIST

Because Paul's life situation is unparalleled, we cannot imitate all he did or his special calling as an apostle to define and defend the gospel. Paul's ministry was a worldwide, itinerate ministry. From the outset, he knew he would be in Ephesus only temporarily, unlike the elders who would be stable, long-term leaders.

Nevertheless, even if you have a family to raise, a job to attend to, and leadership responsibilities in the church, you too, like Paul, must finish the "course" God has set before you to run and the "ministry" you have received from the Lord Jesus.

Scripture instructs all Christian men and women, not just elders, to "be steadfast, immovable, always abounding in the work of the Lord, knowing that in the Lord your labor is not in vain (1 Cor. 15:58)." Also, you are to "present your bodies as a living sacrifice, holy and acceptable to God, which is your spiritual worship" (Rom. 12:1; read also Rom. 6:13, 19, 22; 7:6; 14:7–9; 1 Cor. 7:35; 2 Cor. 5:9–10; 2 Cor. 11:3; Col. 3:23–24).

> You too must finish the "course" God has set before you and the "ministry" you have received from the Lord Jesus.

Putting Christ First

We used to have a neighbor who owned a large, expensive speed-boat, a top-of-the-line camper, and *all* the camping and fishing gear you can imagine. Because he owned his own business, he was able to take every Friday off, and every weekend he would go with his family and friends to the mountains and camp by a lake. From Friday morning until Sunday evening they would jet-ski, fish, hike, eat loads of food, and drink large amounts of beer. It was a whole weekend of partying. Once when we were casually discussing his love for boating and camping, he said with a great deal of emotion, "I live for the weekends!"

Immediately I thought, Paul would have said instead, "I live for Christ!" Granted, there is nothing wrong with camping, boating, fishing, or eating with family and friends. We all need to enjoy these kinds of relaxing activities. The Lord gives rest and enjoyment to his saints.

> For the disciples of Jesus, life can never
> be self-centered, but Christ-centered, and that
> leads to other-people centeredness.

However, the followers of the Lord Jesus cannot say, "I live for the weekends to party with my family and friends. I live for personal pleasure." That lifestyle would be idolatrous. For the disciples of Jesus, life can never be self-centered. Life must be Christ-centered, which leads to other-people-centeredness. We are to live lives of sacrificial service to God and our neighbor. We are to "bear fruit for God" (Rom. 7:4), "through love serve one another" (Gal. 5:13), and be a people "zealous for good works" (Titus 2:14). This is doubly true for those of us who have positions of leadership in the church.

Be Prepared to Finish Well

Like Paul, you too have a "course" laid out before you to run. We are all runners in the great race of life. The writer of Hebrews makes this point abundantly clear. We are all to "run with endurance the race that is set before us":

> Therefore, since we are surrounded by so great a cloud of witnesses, let us also lay aside every weight, and sin which clings so closely, and let us run with endurance the race that is set before us, looking to Jesus, the founder and perfecter of our faith, who for the joy that was set before him endured the cross, despising the shame, and is seated at the right hand of the throne of God. (Heb. 12:1–2)

This race is a God-appointed race. You are to run with endurance, keeping your mind fixed firmly on the example of Jesus, "who for the joy that was set before him endured the cross, despising the shame." Keep your eyes on Jesus. Run with endurance, so you will "not grow weary or fainthearted" (Heb. 12:3).

A Ministry: Like Paul, you too have a "ministry" prepared by God for you to complete: "For we are his workmanship, *created in Christ Jesus for good works,* which God prepared beforehand, that *we should walk in them*" (Eph. 2:10).

The good works God has prepared for you are to oversee and shepherd his beloved people. This ministry Scripture declares to be a most "noble task" (1 Tim. 3:1).

> "Let us also lay aside every weight, and sin which clings so closely, and let us run with endurance the race that is set before us." Hebrews 12:1

Only One Life

Consider C. T. Studd's thought-provoking poem, "Only One Life." C. T. Studd was born into a wealthy British family, graduated from Cambridge University, and achieved fame as a star cricket player for England. Yet he left wealth, comfort, and fame to become a missionary, as one of the Cambridge Seven who went to China under Hudson Taylor's China Inland Mission (1885). On giving up all for Christ and the gospel he wrote the following inspiring poem:

Two little lines I heard one day,
Traveling along life's busy way;
Bringing conviction to my heart,
And from my mind would not depart;
Only one life, 'twill soon be past,
Only what's done for Christ will last.

Only one life, yes only one,
Soon will its fleeting hours be done;
Then, in 'that day' my Lord to meet,
And stand before His Judgement seat;
Only one life, 'twill soon be past,
Only what's done for Christ will last.

Only one life, the still small voice,
Gently pleads for a better choice
Bidding me selfish aims to leave,
And to God's holy will to cleave;
Only one life, 'twill soon be past,
Only what's done for Christ will last.

Only one life, a few brief years,
Each with its burdens, hopes, and fears;
Each with its [days] I must fulfill,
Living for self or in His will;
Only one life, 'twill soon be past,
Only what's done for Christ will last.

When this bright world would tempt me sore,
When Satan would a victory score;
When self would seek to have its way,
Then help me Lord with joy to say;
Only one life, 'twill soon be past,
Only what's done for Christ will last.

Give me Father, a purpose deep,
In joy or sorrow Thy word to keep;

Faithful and true what e'er the strife,
Pleasing Thee in my daily life;
Only one life, 'twill soon be past,
Only what's done for Christ will last.

Oh let my love with fervor burn,
And from the world now let me turn;
Living for Thee, and Thee alone,
Bringing Thee pleasure on Thy throne;
Only one life, 'twill soon be past,
Only what's done for Christ will last.

Only one life, yes only one,
Now let me say, "Thy will be done";
And when at last I'll hear the call,
I know I'll say, "'Twas worth it all";
Only one life, 'twill soon be past,
Only what's done for Christ will last.[12]

KEY POINTS TO REMEMBER

1. Our Lord must be first, our preeminent, central focus, controlling everything we do and are: "Only one life, 'twill soon be past; only what's done for Christ will last."

2. Grasp the logic of the following two declarations: "If Jesus Christ be God and died for me, then no sacrifice can be too great for me to make for Him." "Love so amazing, so divine, demands my soul, my life, my all." Is that your testimony?

3. Prepare yourself so that you know well and are able to defend well the biblical teaching of salvation by God's grace alone, through Christ alone, through faith alone.

4. No one should ever be appointed a church elder who does not know the gospel well and is not able and willing to defend the gospel of the grace of God.

5. No matter what your life situation is, you are to finish the course God has set before you and the ministry you have received from the Lord Jesus to shepherd God's flock.

---

[1] Norman Grubb, *C. T. Studd: Cricketer and Pioneer* (Fort Washington, PA: Christian Literature Crusade, 1933), 132.

[2] Gordon Fee, *Paul's Letter to the Philippians*, NICNT (Grand Rapids: Eerdmans, 1995), 227.

[3] This is a quote from one of Eric Alexander's sermons. However, I am not able to locate the source.

[4] BDAG, s.v. "διαμαρτύρομαι," 233, "to make a solemn declaration about the truth of something, testify of, bear witness to (originally under oath)." The term can also carry the idea "to exhort with authority in matters of extraordinary importance."

[5] In his letters Paul uses the noun *gospel* sixty times and the verb form (εὐαγγελίζω [*euangelizō*]) 21 times. In Acts, the noun (εὐαγγέλιον [*euangelion*]) is only used here in Acts 20:24 and 15:7 ("the word of the gospel"). The verb, however, "to preach or announce the gospel" is used fifteen times in Acts. This is a term familiar to those who know the Old Testament book of Isaiah: "How beautiful upon the mountains are the feet of him who brings good news, who publishes peace, who brings good news of happiness, who publishes salvation, who says to Zion, 'Your God reigns'" (Isa. 52:7; also Isa. 40:9–11; 61:1–3).

[6] Sam Storms, "The Gospel," in *The ESV Systematic Theology Study Bible*, ed. Christopher W. Morgan, Stephen J. Wellum, and Robert A. Peterson (Wheaton, IL: Crossway, 2017), 1707.

[7] *NIDNTTE*, s.v. "εὐαγγέλιον," 2:310:

> As used by Paul, however, εὐαγγέλιον (*euangelion*) does not mean only the content of what is preached, but also the act, process, and execution of the proclamation. Content and process of preaching are inseparable (cf. Rom. 1:1; 1 Cor. 9:14, 18). For in the very act of proclamation its content becomes reality and brings about the salvation it communicates. 'The gospel does not merely bear witness to salvation history; it is itself salvation history' (G. Friedrich, s.v. "εὐαγγέλιον," *TDNT*, 2:731).

The term εὐαγγέλιον, then, connotes the act of proclamation or the preaching of the good news. Since *gospel* is good news that must be told, both the content of the news and the act of communicating that content are inseparable.

[8] BDAG, s.v. "χάρις," 1080 ["grace"], "The proclamation of salvation is the message of divine beneficence." *NIDNTTE*, s.v. "χάρις," 4:658: "In Pauline teaching *charis* denotes the essence of God's decisive saving act in Jesus Christ, which took place in his sacrificial death, and also of all its consequences in the present and future (Rom. 3:24–26)."

[9] Gordon D. Fee, *The First Epistle to the Corinthians*, NICNT (Grand Rapids: Eerdmans, 2014), 927.

[10] *NIDNTTE*, s.v. "χάρις," 4:658.

[11] This illustration is adapted from H. A. Ironside, *In the Heavenlies: Practical Expository Addresses on the Epistle to the Ephesians* (Neptune, NJ: Loizeaux, 1937; repr. 1975), 60.

[12] Readers can access the poem at: https://paulhockley.com/2016/05/24/quote-only-one-life-twill-soon-be-past-poem-by-c-t-studd/.

CHAPTER 6

Declaring the Whole Counsel of God

*And now, behold, I know that none of you among whom
I have gone about proclaiming the kingdom will see my face again.
Therefore I testify to you this day that I am innocent of the blood of all,
for I did not shrink from declaring to you the whole counsel of God.*
(Acts 20:25–27)

The phrase "And now, behold" marks another transition in the speech. Here Paul directly announces that none of his dear co-workers will see his face again. These men deeply loved Paul, so to hear that they would not see him again was heart-wrenching.

Luke recorded their tender, emotional parting:

And there was much weeping on the part of all; they embraced Paul and kissed him, being sorrowful most of all because of the word he had spoken, that they would not see his face again. (Acts 20:37–38)

The words, "none of you . . . will see my face again" sets the tone for the entire discourse. The content chosen for the address fits the nature of a farewell message by the founder and apostle of the church. This was a decisive moment in the history of the first church in the city of Ephesus, which became one of the most influential churches of the first century.

PROCLAIMING THE KINGDOM OF GOD

The men who sat before Paul had had the extraordinary privilege of repeatedly hearing Paul "proclaiming the kingdom." The verb for "proclaiming" means "to make public declaration, proclaim aloud."[1] In fact, Paul refers to himself as a "herald,"[2] personally appointed by Christ to publicly proclaim aloud the way of entrance into God's eternal kingdom. One of the older commentators writes, "With great force and brevity [these words] express Paul's consciousness that he is the herald of a king and of his kingdom."[3] The public proclamation of the kingdom of God for both unbelievers and believers was a central aspect of Paul's preaching. It included both the nature of the kingdom of God and the conditions for entrance.

> Again we see the emphasis on Paul's teaching
> and proclamation ministry.

Here again we see the emphasis on Paul's teaching and proclamation ministry. His life was dedicated to communicating God's message of redemption through the death and resurrection of Jesus to all who will hear and believe.

Entrance into the Kingdom

The kingdom of God is a major theme in the Bible. Proclaiming the kingdom of God involves preaching both the message of salvation in Christ alone and the glorious truths regarding God's kingdom program.

A basic, critical question arises when the kingdom of God is proclaimed: How does one enter God's kingdom? Both Jesus and Paul taught that it is by the new birth—not by natural birth, or family privilege, or ethnicity, or law-keeping. As Paul put it: "I tell you this, brothers: flesh and blood cannot inherit the kingdom of God" (1 Cor. 15:50). "Unless one is born again," declared Jesus, "he cannot see the kingdom of God" (John 3:3). The gospel message explains the only way to enter and inherit "the kingdom of Christ and God" (Eph. 5:5). But there is also a serious warning that those who profess Jesus but persist in practicing the works of the flesh "will not inherit the kingdom of God" (Gal. 5:21; also Eph. 5:5; 1 Cor. 6:9).

Paul's Love for the Lord's Return

Proclaiming the kingdom of God includes both the gospel-salvation message and the broader subject of eschatology. Paul loved to speak and write of the victorious return of Jesus Christ and how this truth should affect our present thinking and daily decisions.

Teaching Eschatology to New Believers: When Paul taught new believers, he did not neglect the subject of eschatology. Eschatology is the study of last things, the end time events of human history. He held back nothing that was profitable for their total understanding of their Christian faith. For example, when he taught the new Christians in the city of Thessalonica—believers who were only weeks or months old in the faith—he taught them eschatology. He writes: *"We do not want you to be uninformed, brothers,"* meaning uninformed about end-time events (1 Thess. 4:13).

PROPHETIC TRUTHS FOR NEW CHRISTIANS

Paul taught the new believers about the glorious return of the Lord Jesus from heaven (1 Thess. 1:10; 2:19; 3:13; 4:15, 16; 5:23; 2 Thess. 1:7; 2:1, 8); being with their Lord at his victorious

---

coming "with his mighty angels in flaming fire" (1 Thess. 3:13; 4:14; 2 Thess. 1:10; 2:1); meeting the Lord in the air at the resurrection (1 Thess. 4:17); deliverance from the wrath of God to come (1 Thess. 1:10; 5:9); the bodily resurrection of believers from the dead (1 Thess. 4:16–17); our eternal future with the Lord (1 Thess. 4:17; 5:10); judgment upon unbelievers at his coming (1 Thess. 5:3; 2 Thess. 1:8; 2:1–12); the final glorification of believers (2 Thess. 2:14); the Day of the Lord (1 Thess. 5:2; 2 Thess. 2:2); eternal judgment (2 Thess. 1:9); the coming of the antichrist and his utter destruction by Christ (2 Thess. 2:3–9). As Paul reminded them later, "Do you not remember that when I [Paul] was still with you I told you these things?" (2 Thess. 2:5).

The following prophetic words to both the Thessalonians and Corinthians should give us all goosebumps. They are God-guaranteed promises:

For the Lord himself will descend from heaven with a cry of command, with the voice of an archangel, and with the sound of the trumpet of God. And the dead in Christ will rise first. Then we who are alive, who are left, will be caught up together with them in the clouds to meet the Lord in the air, and so we will always be with the Lord. (1 Thess. 4:16–17)

Behold! I tell you a mystery. We shall not all sleep, but we shall all be changed, in a moment, in the twinkling of an eye, at the last trumpet. For the trumpet will sound, and the dead will be raised imperishable, and we shall be changed. For this perishable body must put on the imperishable, and this mortal body must put on immortality. When the perishable puts on the imperishable, and the mortal puts on immortality, then shall come to pass this saying that is written: "Death is swallowed up in victory." "O death, where is your victory? O death, where is your sting?" (1 Cor. 15:51–55; also Rom. 8:11, 23)

This is certain: The Lord wants all his people to know about their heavenly citizenship and to anticipate his return from heaven, at which time Jesus will transform our earthly bodies to be like his glorious resurrected body:

> But our citizenship is in heaven, and from it we await a Savior, the Lord Jesus Christ, who will transform our lowly body to be like his glorious body, by the power that enables him even to subject all things to himself. (Phil. 3:20–21; see also Rom. 6:5, 9)

Be Prepared to Explain and Proclaim End-Time Events

As instructors in sound doctrine you should be able to use the prophetic Scriptures to exhort, comfort, encourage, and educate the people under your pastoral care, just as Paul did. "Therefore encourage one another with these words" (1 Thess. 4:18).

> As comforters of the Lord's people, you should know and use the prophetic Scriptures in your pastoral ministry to people.

When helping people face their own death or the deaths of loved ones, we can say with assurance that we believers do "not grieve as others do who have no hope" (1 Thess. 4:13). We have a glorious hope in the promise of Jesus's return, the bodily resurrection, and "entrance into the eternal kingdom of our Lord and Savior Jesus Christ (2 Peter 1:11). As comforters of the Lord's people, you should know and use the prophetic Scriptures in your pastoral ministry.

Evangelism

Paul used the good news about the kingdom of God as an integral part of his evangelistic message.[4] People are naturally curious about the future, especially about life after death. Many people have come to Christ as a result of hearing God's future prophetic program preached from the Bible.

Love for Bible Prophecy

Do not be afraid of Bible prophecy or of debated prophetic issues. It is the Word of the Lord! It is part of "the whole counsel of God." Bible teachers cannot be biblically illiterate about, or disinterested in, God's prophetic program. You should want to know what God has planned for his people in the future. Those who love the Bible should love Bible prophecy and be willing to proclaim it as did Paul and Jesus.

Although there is disagreement over some of the details of Bible prophecy, there is agreement on the fundamentals of prophesy, such as the return of the Lord Jesus, the bodily resurrection, the final judgment, defeat of Satan, and the new earth and heavens: "All things new" (Rev. 21:5).

There are many good books explaining the differences between Premillennialism, Amillennialism, and Postmillennialism. You should know the issues and have relevant Scriptures in mind when questioned. Be like the Berean Jews, "examining the Scriptures daily to see if these things were so" (Acts 17:11).

THE WATCHMAN'S RESPONSIBILITY TO DELIVER THE WORD OF THE LORD

Many times in the past, the Ephesian elders had heard Paul publicly proclaim the gospel of the grace of God and the kingdom of God. But now this would all change, for he tells them that they will not "see his face again." He will not teach among them again or be with them to give his personal counsel.

This crucial statement is followed with the conjunction "therefore" (v. 26). Because they will not see his face again, "therefore" he testifies solemnly before them that he is "innocent of the blood of all." Although he was leaving, Paul would be innocent of their spiritual deaths, should any of the people under his teaching perish in their sins. If any of them were not adequately equipped to protect God's church from heretical doctrines, this was not Paul's fault. This is because he had not failed to proclaim the Word of the Lord to them in its entirety while he was with them.

The Watchman on the Wall

The concept of being "innocent of the blood of all" reaches back to the Old Testament imagery of the watchman on the city wall. There were no satellites in space or radar systems in the ancient days to guard a city. The watchman was responsible for guarding a city from invaders. He was charged with watching and listening for any impending danger, and then to sound the alarm warning the people to take action.

Imagine an invading army approaching a small city quietly in the dark of night, to plunder its goods and kidnap or kill its people. But the watchman is sound asleep or preoccupied with some trivial, personal matter. When the army attacks the city, no warning alarm is sounded, and the people are killed in their sleep. Who is responsible for this disaster? The distracted watchman is responsible for the death (= the blood) of all those who perish. His punishment for being asleep and not sounding the alarm is his own death (= his blood).

Using the watchman imagery, God said to the prophet Ezekiel:

> So you, son of man, I have made a *watchman* for the house of Israel. Whenever you hear a word from my mouth, *you shall give them warning from me.* If I say to the wicked, O wicked one, you shall surely die, and you do not speak to warn the wicked to turn from his way, that wicked person shall die in his iniquity, but *his blood I will require at your hand.* But if you warn the wicked to turn from his way, and he does not turn from his way, that person shall die in his iniquity, but you will have delivered your soul. (Ezek. 33:7–9; see also 3:17–21; 33:1–6)

In Acts 18, we read that, while in Corinth,

> Paul was occupied with the word, testifying to the Jews that Christ was Jesus. And when they opposed and reviled him, he shook out his garments and said to them, "Your blood be on your own heads! *I am innocent.* From now on I will go to the Gentiles." (Acts 18:5–6)

An Innocent Man: Like the prophet Ezekiel, Paul had faithfully delivered and taught the Lord's salvation message to the people. There was no blood-guilt on his hands. He could testify[5] solemnly before God and before the Ephesian elders that he was "innocent of the blood of all." No one could say of Paul, "You did not tell me the Word of the Lord."

Vigilant: Paul was a vigilant watchman, teaching both in public and in private (v. 20), "testifying both to Jews and to Greeks of repentance toward God and our faith in our Lord Jesus Christ" (v. 21). He *fulfilled* the "ministry" he had received from the Lord Jesus, "to testify to the gospel of the grace of God" (v. 24). The Ephesian elders had heard him many times boldly proclaim the kingdom of God to all people (v. 25). So, although these church leaders would not see his face again, they could never claim that they were not warned of the dangers ahead, that they had not been taught the full message of God's salvation in Christ, or that they had not been *prepared by Paul for their shepherding task.*

Be Prepared to Keep Watch Over God's Flock

If you are a church elder, God has made you a watchman over the souls of his people. If you do not deliver God's full message to your people, their blood will be required of you. If you compromise his message out of fear or any other reason, you will have blood-guilt upon your hands.

You have the solemn responsibility to tell the full gospel message to all those in your charge. You are responsible to sound the alarm when sheep-eating wolves are coming. You are God's watchman, and you will someday stand before him to give an account for your service as a watchman of his people:

> Obey your leaders and submit to them, for *they are keeping watch over your souls*, as those who will have to *give an account*. Let them do this with joy and not with groaning, for that would be of no advantage to you. (Heb. 13:17)

Blind Watchmen: The prophet Isaiah cried out against Israel's derelict leaders. He called them blind, ignorant, lazy, sleeping watchmen:

> All you beasts of the field, come to devour [in divine judgment]—all you beasts in the forest. His watchmen are blind; they are all without knowledge; they are all silent [watch] dogs; they cannot bark, dreaming, lying down, loving to slumber. . . . They are shepherds who have no understanding; they have all turned to their own way, each to his own gain, one and all. (Isa. 56:9–11)

A blind watchman is as worthless as a blind lifeguard. An inept shepherd is equally useless. Do not be a blind guide or an inept elder who fails to watch over the Lord's redeemed people. If you are a blind and ignorant church elder, soon there will be no church left under your leadership. It will either be devoured by hungry wolves or die of malnutrition.

"His watchmen are blind; they are all without knowledge; they are all silent [watch] dogs. . . . They are shepherds who have no understanding." Isaiah 56:10–11

Revive the Terminology: We don't normally use watchman imagery today in our discussions on pastoral leadership. But we need to revive this concept because it conveys a very apt picture of the task assigned to all shepherd elders: protecting others from soul-threatening spiritual danger. We need to talk more about ourselves as watchmen over the Lord's flock and what this means. How should this thinking influence our work?

You have been placed by the Holy Spirit to be watchmen, for the Spirit knows that sheep-devouring wolves will always be on the alert for vulnerable sheep. Paul is our example. He was a faithful watchman who could say to the church elders, "for three years I did not cease night or day to admonish every one with tears" (v. 31).

> You have been placed by the Holy Spirit
> to be watchmen, for the Spirit knows that
> sheep-devouring wolves will always be on the
> alert for vulnerable sheep.

TEACHING THE WHOLE COUNSEL OF GOD

We come now to one of the most significant statements of the entire discourse. The reason Paul can assert with such confidence that he is "innocent of the blood of all" is: "for I did not shrink from declaring to you the whole counsel of God" (v. 27) The conjunction "for" introduces a reason: Paul was innocent of their blood *because* he consistently and diligently taught them "the whole counsel of God." Other translations of this key phrase are:

- "the whole will of God" (New International Version)
- "the whole plan of God" (Christian Standard Bible)
- "the whole purpose of God" (New American Standard Bible; New Revised Standard Version; NET Bible)

The Whole Plan of God

This is the second time Paul has made this point, and it is a critical aspect of his message. Earlier he reminded the elders that, "I did not shrink from declaring to you anything that was profitable." Here in verse 27 he repeats, "I did not shrink from declaring to you the whole counsel of God." Paul was thorough in "declaring"[6] "the whole counsel of God" to the church and its leaders. He held back no doctrine that was "profitable" to the elders' theological education and complete preparation for their work of protecting and teaching the whole counsel of God.

God's Counsel: The term "counsel" here refers to the divine sovereign "will," "purpose," or "plan" of God.[7] God's plans are not capricious or unpredictable like those of the ancient Greek gods. They are based on divine intention and determination, available for our intelligent, thoughtful deliberation. The God of the Bible knows the beginning and the end of human history and everything in between, because he has determined it, and it will unfold according to his own purpose, just as Isaiah the prophet eloquently states:

> "For I am God, and there is no other; I am God, and there is none like me, declaring the end from the beginning and from ancient times things not yet done, saying, '*My counsel shall stand*, and I will accomplish all my purpose,' calling a bird of prey from the east, the man of my counsel from a far country. I have spoken, and I will bring it to pass; *I have purposed*, and I will do it." (Isa. 46:9–11)

The "Whole" Counsel: Attached to the determinative counsel of God is the significant little word "whole" or "all." It is the whole plan and purpose of God that Paul taught. He did not shrink from teaching anything that was necessary for the Ephesian elders to know about the divine sovereign plan and purpose of God. He did not teach just parts of the plan of God, or emphasize his favorite doctrines, or dwell on only the non-offensive parts. He declared the "whole" plan of God, everything that was "profitable."

Paul makes a very important claim here. Such thorough teaching of the whole of God's plan would help deter false teachers from later alleging that only they possessed the secret teachings of Paul that he did not reveal to others while in Ephesus. But there are no secret teachings of Paul. Paul had declared the whole counsel of God to all who would hear and believe, the very gospel taught him by the Lord Jesus Christ.

> The Ephesian elders had the best seminary training possible from the best teacher possible.

The Storyline of the Bible and Its Doctrines: The whole counsel of God includes the entire storyline of the Bible, from Genesis 1:1 to Revelation 22, and all major Bible doctrines. From Genesis to Revelation, from Adam to Christ, the Bible presents a coherent story, God's master plan of his sovereign, redemptive purposes. In his letter to the Ephesians, Paul reminds the believers that God "works all things according to the *counsel* of his will" (Eph. 1:11).

Paul was thorough and persistent in teaching the "whole counsel of God." As a result, the Ephesian elders had the best seminary training possible from the best teacher possible. They were not ignorant of gospel truths or of Christian doctrine.

Paul never accommodated Christ's teachings to the culture of the time or to the spirit of the age. Because he declared only the Word of the Lord and in its entirety, Paul could assert: "I am innocent of the blood of all."

Be Prepared to Teach the Whole Counsel of God

As God's shepherds of God's flock, you too need to teach "the whole counsel of God." Of all the duties involved in shepherding people, teaching the great and glorious truths of Scripture is the most gratifying and enjoyable. It is also most profitable for the people. Seeing believers grow in their faith is one of the great joys of the shepherding ministry.

> Of all the duties involved in shepherding people,
> teaching the great and glorious truths of Scripture
> is the most gratifying and enjoyable.

The Secular Tsunami

As a result of our increasingly secular society, our over-busy lifestyles, and the intrusion of the ubiquitous entertainment industry into our homes, the Bible has become a foreign book for many. Most people do not know the whole story of redemption, from the beginning of the Bible to the end. They have no idea how the books of the Bible fit together. They have little knowledge of who Abraham, Moses, David, or Jeremiah were, or the covenants God made with them. Thus, they do not understand or appreciate the magisterial epistles of Romans, Galatians, and Hebrews.

Hollywood vs. Scripture: Our young people know more about the stars of Hollywood and their movies than they do about the godly patriarchs of the Old Testament or the earthly life of Christ. This is a fact! They are so secularized that their powers of spiritual discernment have been dulled. If our youth do read the Scriptures, it is through the lens of secular dogma, not through a mind confident in the authority and truthfulness of God-breathed Scripture.

A secular tsunami is washing over our churches and our young people, the next generation of leaders. As God's watchmen, you must sound the alarm, lest they be swept away. If we do not warn our people of this secular tidal wave, we will have to answer for their blood. In our church, there is a poster in the youth area that reads, "If we don't teach our children to follow Christ, the world will teach them not to." This is an apt warning for us all to heed.

Unlike any other time in modern history, we need to continually encourage our people to daily read the Scriptures, study the Scriptures individually and in groups, and memorize Scripture. The Word of God is the life-sustaining, divine bread of heaven for our nourishment.

When Jesus was in the wilderness, the devil repeatedly tempted him to disobey the will of God. But each time, Jesus used Scripture to refute the devil. He met each temptation to veer from God's purposes with "For it is written." We need to do the same.

Heed the good advice of A. W. Tozer about the danger of anything that keeps us from reading and studying the very words of God:

> Whatever keeps me from the Bible is my enemy, however harmless it may appear to be. Whatever engages my attention when I should be meditating on God and things eternal does injury to my soul. Let the cares of life crowd out the Scriptures from my mind and I have suffered loss where I can least afford it. Let me accept anything else instead of the Scriptures and I have been cheated and robbed to my eternal confusion.[8]

GOOD RESOURCES AVAILABLE

We are blessed by the fact that there are many resources available today to help Christians grow in their faith. Excellent books explain in simple terms the full biblical story of redemption. Audio messages by outstanding preachers and daily podcasts by our best Christian leaders and thinkers are easily accessible. Make these resources readily available for the people in your church. Encourage your people to use these resources to grow in the knowledge of God and his Word.

Example: In the days before personal computers, iPhones, and podcasts, our church provided hundreds of free audio cassettes from the world's best Bible expositors. We encouraged our congregation to listen to these when they were driving in their cars, while exercising, or during their personal study time. This ministry did much to advance our people in the knowledge of God and Scripture, and it generated many profitable discussions in home groups and Bible studies.

At the end of my seminary education, I had to take the oral exam with one of the school's professors. I had my exam with a professor who was gracious and humorous. We had a wonderful time together discussing Scripture. He was genuinely interested in what I believed and why, as we had some conflicting beliefs. It turned out to be a very pleasant experience. After the exam, later that day, a fellow student told me that the professor and he had talked. The professor said to the student that my exam was one of the best he had ever experienced.

I knew that what we had talked about and my answers from the Bible to his questions came largely from that knowledge of Scripture, Bible doctrine, and apologetics that had come from the past four years by listening every day to the world's greatest Bible teachers and apologists. While in my car driving, while exercising, while preparing for study, I had listened to hundreds, maybe thousands, of hours of Bible teaching.

I tell you this story in order to help you realize that you can get a free Bible school education over a five-year period if you will consistently listen to Spirit-gifted Bible teachers on the books of Romans, Ephesians, Galatians, Hebrews, as well as the other New Testament and Old Testament books. Listen also to the eminent Christian apologists for the faith that God has graciously given to his people.

"The failure to teach truth eventually leads to failure
of Christ's people even to know the truth."
—R. Albert Mohler

A Plan: As Spirit-appointed shepherds, you have the responsibility of teaching the whole plan of God to your flock. An earlier comment made by R. Albert Mohler bears repeating: "The failure to teach truth eventually leads to failure of Christ's people even to know the truth."[9]

Surveys of the biblical beliefs of professing Christians support Mohler's assertion. Ligonier Ministries' State of Theology survey asked Americans about their beliefs about Jesus, salvation, and the Bible. Fifty-two percent agreed with the statement that "Jesus was a great teacher, but he was not God." More shocking is the result that 30 percent of Evangelicals agreed that Christ was merely a great teacher. More than 48 percent agreed with the statement that "The Bible, like all sacred writings, contains helpful accounts of ancient myths but is not literally true." Nearly one half of professing Evangelical Christians affirm some notion of religious pluralism (the statement reads, "God accepts the worship of all religions, including Christianity, Judaism, and Islam").

The survey's conclusion is that Evangelicals "seem to be influenced by the culture's uncertainty about what truth is, who Jesus is, and how sinners are saved."[10]

> It is your duty to feed the flock and "to equip the saints for the work of ministry [service]."

How are shepherds to combat "the culture's uncertainty" about the truth and protect our flocks? Practically speaking, you need to consult together as elders about your church's teaching ministry and develop a plan. You need to know what you are doing, and let the people know what you are doing. It is your duty to feed the flock and "to equip the saints for the work of ministry [service], for building up the body of Christ" (Eph. 4:12). Do not leave the people in ignorance or ill-equipped to serve the body of Christ.

Many churches all over the world have discovered that systematic, expository Bible teaching every Sunday morning is the very best way to ensure that the believing community is instructed in the whole counsel of God. Of course, home Bible studies, small group studies in Bible doctrine, and new believers' Bible classes are all needed as well to educate people in the knowledge of God and Christ.

Good Books: Another way to help educate your people is to recommend good books for them to read. The founder of what later became known as Methodism, John Wesley, wrote: "It cannot be that the people should grow in grace unless they give themselves to reading. A reading people will always be a knowing people.[11]

Have a display of recommended books that the elders feel the congregation should read. You do not need to get into the bookselling business; it will be sufficient to have copies on display and let the people order the books on their own.

> "It cannot be that the people should grow in grace unless they give themselves to reading. A reading people will always be a knowing people." —John Wesley

A sad fact is that our society is being dumbed down by countless hours of movie watching. As educators, *continually encourage your people to read and not just watch movies or sports.* We should say with the psalmist, "Turn my eyes from looking at worthless things, and give me life in your ways" (Ps. 119:37). If you find reading difficult (and many people do), listen to audio books. This is a powerful tool for absorbing good Christian literature to help expand your mind and enrich your character.

However you do this, be sure that you are doing everything possible to fulfill the solemn responsibility that God has entrusted to you to teach your people "the whole counsel of God." This is the goal of faithful watchmen, shepherds, and overseers. As Paul said to Timothy:

If you put these things before the brothers [and sisters], you will be a good servant of Christ Jesus, being trained in the words of the faith and of the good doctrine that you have followed. (1 Tim. 4:6)

Helpful Resources

Two Important Recommendations: Albert Mohler, Jr., *The Gathering Storm: Secularism, Culture, and the Church* (Nashville, TN: Thomas Nelson, 2020). Kevin DeYoung, *Taking God at His Word: Why the Bible Is Knowable, Necessary, and Enough, and What that Means for You and Me* (Wheaton, IL: Crossway, 2014). Also available in audio form.

KEY POINTS TO REMEMBER

1. You should be able to use the prophetic Word of Scripture to exhort, comfort, encourage, and educate those under your shepherding care.

2. You are God's watchmen over the precious souls of God's people. Take this responsibility seriously.

3. Know and teach "the whole counsel of God." Do not shrink from declaring anything that is profitable for the flock's spiritual education.

4. Discuss your church's teaching/education ministry and develop a plan. Know what you are doing, and let the people know what you are doing.

5. Continually encourage your people to read and not just watch movies or sports. Also encourage audio messages and books.

6. You are educators.

---

[1] BDAG, s.v. "κηρύσσω," 543; see 1 Cor. 9:27; Gal. 2:2; 2 Tim. 4:2; also *NIDNTTE*, s.v. "κηρύσσω," 2:674–681 (esp. 677–81).

[2] A "herald" (Gr. κῆρυξ [*kēryx*], "hear ye, hear ye") 1 Tim. 2:7; 2 Tim. 1:11; see also Acts 17:18 where Paul is described by the Athenians as a "preacher [or "proclaimer," καταγγελεύς (*katangeleus*)] of foreign divinities."

[3] G. V. Lechler, "The Acts of the Apostles," trans. C. F. Schaeffer, in *Commentary on the Holy Scriptures*, ed. John Peter Lange (1866; repr. Grand Rapids: Zondervan, 1960), 9:374.

[4] Acts 8:12; 19:8; 28:23, 30–31.

[5] BDAG, s.v. "μαρτύρομαι," 619, "to affirm something with solemnity, testify, bear witness"; also Gal. 5:3; Eph. 4:17.

[6] BDAG, s.v. "ἀναγγέλλω," 59, "to provide information, disclose, announce, proclaim, teach."

[7] BDAG, s.v. "βουλή," 182, "of the divine will;" "The βουλή fills the whole content of the apostolic preaching" (Gottlob Schrenk, "βουλή," in *TDNT*, 1:635; also *NIDNTTE*, s.v. "βούλομαι," 1:526–530 (esp. 528–30). For the divine counsel or plan (βουλή, *boule*), see Luke 7:30; Acts 2:23; 13:36; 20:27; Heb. 6:17; the divine "purpose" (προθεσμια, *prothesmia*): Eph. 1:11; 3:11 (eternal purpose), Rom. 8:28; 9:11; 2 Tim. 1:9.

[8] A. W. Tozer, *That Incredible Christian* (Harrisburg, PA: Christian Publications, 1964), 82.

[9] R. Albert Mohler, Jr., *The Gathering Storm: Secularism, Culture, and the Church* (Nashville, TN: Nelson Books, 2020), 22.

[10] https://thestateoftheology.com/

[11] John Wesley, *The Message of the Wesleys: A Reader of Instruction and Devotion*, compiled by Philip S. Watson (London: Epworth Press, 1964), 183.

CHAPTER 7

Pay Strict Attention to Yourselves and All God's Flock

Pay careful attention to yourselves and to all the flock, in which the Holy Spirit has made you overseers, to care for [to shepherd] the church of God, which he obtained with his own blood.
(Acts 20:28)

I know that after my departure fierce wolves will come in among you, not sparing the flock; and from among your own selves will arise men speaking twisted things, to draw away the disciples after them.
(Acts 20:30)

After reminding the elders of his own life and ministry, Paul then gives them a direct charge. This is the first exhortation of the speech. Paul knew that although he had taught the elders "the whole counsel of God," if they were not vigilant, they could still be deceived and led astray by the masters of deception, the archenemies of the Church of Jesus Christ—the false teachers. Hence, his exhortation: "Pay careful attention to yourselves and to all the flock."

> Once more, Paul's high view of the church's elders,
> and their indispensable role of protecting God's flock
> from wolves, is highlighted.

I cannot emphasize enough the theological and practical importance of this apostolic, prophetic charge. This exhortation is foundational to our understanding of the role of New Testament, Christian elders (vv. 28–31). We would be seriously mistaken to approach this passage by simply arguing over its literary structure, debating the accuracy of Luke's reporting, or finding other problems with the passage. Paul's message is crystal clear and a matter of life and death to all local churches: *Guard yourselves and all God's flock because sheep-eating wolves are coming! Be alert! Be vigilant! Be prepared!* It doesn't get more serious than that! Once more, Paul's high view of the church's elders, and their indispensable role of protecting God's flock from wolves, is highlighted.

PAY CLOSE ATTENTION TO YOURSELVES

We now come to the main exhortation of the speech. If the church is to survive the attacks of "fierce wolves" (v. 29), the elders must pay strict attention to their own spiritual state before God, as well as to all the members of the flock under their charge.

First Paul tells the elders to "pay careful attention to yourselves." The verb for "pay careful attention" means "to be in a state of alert, be concerned about, care for, take care,"[1] or "take thought for."[2] The *New American Standard Bible* and the *Christian Standard Bible* translate the verb as "be on guard." The *New International Version* and the *New Revised Standard Version* translate the verb as "keep watch over"; the *New King James Version* has "take heed."

This verb is an imperative verb of command, and the tense indicates continuous action. In other words, Paul was saying, keep a constant watch over yourselves: Don't be inattentive or preoccupied with lesser things. Be watchful! Be attentive! Be on guard! Also, this verb is used several times in the context of false teaching.[3] For instance, Jesus warned his disciples, "Beware of false prophets, who come to you in sheep's clothing but inwardly are ravenous wolves" (Matt. 7:15; see also Matt. 24:11, 24–25).[4] Like Jesus, Paul warned his coworkers of the inevitable dangers of "fierce wolves."

Do Not Miss the First Order of Business

What Paul says first is easy to miss: "Pay careful attention to yourselves." We tend to skip quickly over these words to what appears to be more important: "Pay careful attention . . . to all the flock." But this is not what the apostle says. The elders are responsible to *first* guard their own spiritual lives, both individually and as a body of elders. This takes effort, self-discipline, desire, thought, prayer, and obedience to God's Word. It also takes an environment of honest, open group accountability between the elders.

You might ask, "As a church elder, what do I do?" First, take seriously your own spiritual state before God. Be attentive to your spiritual growth, your daily walk with Christ, your moral integrity, and your biblical and theological beliefs. My dear friends, this is your first duty before God and your congregation.

Soul Care Comes First

Paying careful attention to yourself is often called "soul care," "self-watch," or "self-shepherding." A. W. Tozer humorously confesses: "Do you know who gives me the most trouble? Do you know who I pray for the most in my pastoral work? Just myself."[5] Proverbs aptly states the point: "Keep your heart with all vigilance, for from it flow the springs of life" (Prov. 4:23). To Timothy, his son in the faith, Paul gave similar instruction:

Keep a close watch on yourself and on the teaching. Persist in this, for by so doing you will save both yourself and your hearers. (1 Tim. 4:16)

Timothy is to persist in keeping "a close watch on"[6] his own personal moral and spiritual character and his public teaching ministry. Through such deliberate thought and effort to maintain the high quality of his Christian life and teaching ministry, he will secure for himself and his hearers salvation in its fullest sense.

> You prove that you are able to keep careful watch over God's flock by first demonstrating that you are diligently watching over your own spiritual life.

Pastoral elders cannot watch over the spiritual lives of others if they do not first know how to guard their own souls. Matthew Henry spurs our thinking: "Those are not likely to be skillful or faithful keepers of the vineyards of others who do not keep their own."[7] You prove that you are able to keep careful watch over God's flock by first demonstrating that you are diligently watching over your own spiritual life.

The Enemy Has a Special Eye on You

In his classic work *The Reformed Pastor*, the well-known Puritan writer Richard Baxter sounded the alarm: Satan "has a special eye on" the leaders of the church. Satan knows that if he can destroy the shepherds, he can swiftly invade and devour the flock:

> Take heed to yourselves because the tempter will make his first and sharpest attack on you. . . . He knows what devastation he is likely to make among the rest if he can make the leaders fall before their eyes. He has long practiced fighting,

neither against great nor small, comparatively, but against the shepherds—that he might scatter the flock. . . . Take heed, then, for the enemy has a special eye on you. You are sure to have his most subtle insinuations, incessant solicitations and violent assaults. Take heed to yourselves, lest he outwit you. The devil is a greater scholar than you are, and a more nimble disputant. . . . And whenever he prevails against you, he will make you the instrument of your own ruin. . . . Do not allow him to use you as the Philistines used Samson—first to deprive you of your strength, then [to] put out your eyes, and finally to make you the subject of his triumph and derision.[8]

If you don't believe in or understand "the spiritual forces of evil" you are not going to last long as an effective shepherd of God's people.

Spiritual warfare is real, and you are on the front line of attack in a war, "against the authorities, against the cosmic powers over this present darkness, against the spiritual forces of evil in the heavenly places" (Eph. 6:12). If you do not believe in or understand "the spiritual forces of evil" you are not going to last long as an effective shepherd of God's people. Martin Luther knew this fact from personal experience, and voiced it so brilliantly in his hymn "A Mighty Fortress Is Our God":

For still our ancient foe doth seek to work us woe;
His craft and power are great,
And armed with cruel hate,
On earth is not his equal.

"Take heed, then, for the enemy has a special eye on you."[9]

HOW TO CARE FOR YOUR SOUL

Here are a few basic disciplines for guarding your spiritual life.

Guard Yourself Against Spiritual Stagnation: Be a Growing Christian

One of the best ways to guard your soul is to be regularly growing in your knowledge of God and Scripture, and in your personal relationship with Christ.

The simple fact is this: You are either growing in Christ or you are stagnating spiritually. If you are drifting spiritually you are drifting away from Christ and into the powerful currents of this secularized world. No one drifts into godliness. "Rather," as Paul told Timothy, "train yourself for godliness" (1 Tim. 4:7).

> Create a positive atmosphere among the elders that encourages continuous learning and growth.

In their book, *Connecting: The Mentoring Relationships You Need to Succeed in Life,* Paul Stanley and Robert Clinton have put their fingers on one of the primary reasons why many Christian leaders and teachers do not finish their lives for Christ well. At some point they stop growing in knowledge and love for Christ:

> We have observed that most people cease learning by the age of forty. By that we mean they no longer actively pursue knowledge, understanding, and experience that will enhance their capacity to grow and contribute to others. Most simply rest on what they already know. But those who finish well maintain a *positive learning attitude* all their lives.[10]

Be zealous about your spiritual growth as a disciple of Jesus Christ. "Do not be slothful in zeal," says Paul, "be fervent in spirit, serve the

Lord" (Rom. 12:11). We are to be lifelong students in God's school of discipleship. For the Christian, school days are never over. So create a positive atmosphere among the elders that encourages continuous learning and growth. Read the following passages of Scripture: 2 Cor. 4:16; Phil. 3:13b–14; 2 Thess. 1:3; 1 Tim. 4:7–8; 4:15; Heb. 5:11–12; 1 Peter 2:2; 2 John 8; Jude 20.

To be engaged in continuous learning and education, you need to become a spiritual sponge. Make the study of Scripture a priority and passion in your life. Don't be like the Christians who "became dull of hearing" the great and glorious truths of biblical Christianity (Heb. 5:11).

Guard Your Mind from False Teaching

Michael Green reminds us that "error has many attractive faces by which even the most experienced may be beguiled."[11] To qualify for pastoral oversight, a presbyter must hold tenaciously to apostolic doctrine. One of the duties of a biblical elder is to be able "to rebuke those who contradict" sound doctrine (Titus 1:9). Protect yourself from the "many attractive faces" of false teaching.

Make wise choices about what you read and whom you listen to. Be careful about your entertainment choices. Our Western society is so overly focused on entertainment that one American journalist wrote: "If and when American civilization collapses, historians of a future date can look back and sneer, 'They entertained themselves to death.'"[12]

> "Error has many attractive faces by which even the most experienced may be beguiled." —Michael Green

Be discerning about what you watch on TV. The philosophy behind many of these shows is produced by "the prince of the power of the air" (Eph. 2:2), the "god of this world" (2 Cor. 4:4). Paul calls such philosophy the "teachings of demons" (1 Tim. 4:1), which are corrupting the minds of millions of Christians, who are unaware and spiritually asleep:

> You therefore, beloved . . . take care that you are not carried away with the error of lawless people and lose your own stability. But *grow in the grace and knowledge of our Lord and Savior Jesus Christ*. (2 Peter 3:17–18)

Guard Your Sexual Life

Not only do you need to be watchful of what your mind is absorbing intellectually and theologically, you also need to be particularly alert to sexual sin and temptation. In our hyper-sexualized, pornographic world, Satan is winning scores of victories over church leaders. As leaders we need to hold each other accountable and pray regularly for strength to maintain our sexual purity. Most importantly, we need to protect and enrich our marriage relationships.

Excellent resources are available today to help us fight the pornography pandemic that has infected our world. Make these resources readily available to your people. "I urge you," Peter writes, "as sojourners and exiles to abstain from the passions of the flesh, which wage war against your soul" (1 Peter 2:11; also 1 Thess. 4:2–8).

Guard Against Sin

Long ago, John Owen wrote, "Be killing sin, or it will be killing you."[13] Never flirt with sin because you will always lose. "Be sure your sin will find you out" (Num. 32:23).

Keep short accounts with God. When your conscience speaks to you about sin, confess it as soon as possible. Claim the blood of Christ: "If we confess our sins, he is faithful and just to forgive us our sins and to cleanse us from all unrighteousness" (1 John 1:9).

Specifically, guard against spiritual laziness, worldliness, prayerlessness, and lack of integrity. "Put on the Lord Jesus Christ," says Paul, "and make no provision for the flesh, to gratify its desires" (Rom. 13:14).

Two largely overlooked qualifications Paul gives for a biblical elder are "upright" and "holy" (Titus 1:8). An oft-quoted statement by an unknown pastor captures the essence of these qualifications: "My people's greatest need is my personal holiness." In a similar manner, Robert Murray McCheyne wrote, "A holy minister is an awful weapon in the hand of God."[14]

Like Leaders, Like People: If you are being secularized by the world, the church will be secularized. If you are drifting spiritually, the church will drift. If you are stagnant spiritually, the church will become stagnant and dull. If you are lifeless spiritually, the church will be lifeless. In his commentary on Acts, Derek Thomas reminds us of the fact that the congregation rarely rises much above the spiritual lives of their leaders:

> The elders are to keep a watch on their own lives lest they set a bad example to those they shepherd. It is a fact of ministry that the congregations over which we minister hardly ever rise to greater expressions of holiness than that which they see evidenced in the lives of those who oversee the ministry. The shape and contours of godliness will be drawn from the lives of the church's pastors. Moral and spiritual failure on the part of the leadership inevitably produces discouragement and a failure to continue in the lives of the people.[15]

As spiritual shepherds, we cannot afford to be careless about our own spiritual state before God. Instead, be "building yourselves up in your most holy faith and praying in the Holy Spirit, keep[ing] yourselves in the love of God" (Jude 20–21). Remember, we are never alone in our spiritual journey. The grace of God, the Spirit of God, the Word of God, and the people of God are with us always: "The Lord is faithful. He will establish you and guard you against the evil one" (2 Thess. 3:3).

Resource: I recommend *Spiritual Disciplines for the Christian Life* by Donald Whitney.[16] It is an excellent overview of the basic spiritual disciplines of the Christian life. Also see his website, BiblicalSpirituality.org.

PAY STRICT ATTENTION TO ALL THE FLOCK

Just as you are to pay strict attention to your own spiritual relationship with Christ and your theological development, you are also to be watchful over the people God has placed in your care: "Pay careful attention . . . to all the flock" (v. 28).

The Flock

Drawing on a familiar Old Testament image,[17] Paul refers to the people of the local church figuratively as a "flock," that is, a flock of sheep or goats, or a mix of both. The local church as a flock is one of many New Testament metaphors for the church. It communicates ownership, dependence, value, and in this context especially, the need for continuous protective care.

The flock metaphor for the church fits precisely with Paul's prediction of fierce wolves, his charge to shepherd the church of God, and the urgent need for shepherds to be keenly alert to danger.

The Flock of God

In the ancient world, flocks of sheep and goats were highly valued for their wool, milk and cheese, meat, bones, and skins for leather goods. A flock represented wealth. What makes this flock so exceedingly valuable is that it is God's flock. In one of the following clauses of verse 28 "the flock" is designated "the church of God." In a similar context, Peter refers to the local church as "the flock of God" (1 Peter 5:2). The flock is God's precious possession. It is the flock he bought, and that he owns, cares for, and loves. It is of great worth to him. So he expects shepherd elders to guard his flock as if the flock were their very own.

When the newly resurrected Jesus charged Peter to shepherd his sheep, he said, "Tend *my* sheep" (John 21:16). The sheep are the property of Jesus, not of Peter. Peter was Jesus's undershepherd. He had to answer to the Good Shepherd, Jesus, for the condition of the sheep.

In many cases in the ancient world the flock did not belong to the shepherd himself. It belonged to someone else, and the shepherd was a servant of the owner. For example, Jacob was the son-in-law of Laban, and he cared for Laban's sheep. He was answerable to Laban for whatever happened to those sheep. In fact, he had to pay Laban back for any of the sheep that were lost (Gen. 31:39). In our case, the sheep belong to God, but we are to care for his sheep as if they were our own.

> These sheep are the property of the Good Shepherd,
> and he cares deeply if any of them are lost.

Pay Close Attention to the Flock

The well-being of a flock depends primarily on the careful attention and skill of its shepherds. Shepherd elders are charged by Paul to pay careful attention to God's flock. In the chapters ahead, we will look more at what shepherding entails, but here, in brief, are some actions that illustrate an attentive and protective shepherd:

- Know who is in the flock under your care.
- Be with the flock, both individually and when gathered corporately.
- Eat with them; share meals together.
- Know their names and family circumstances.
- Recognize the cultural issues confronting them in their daily lives.
- Observe their spiritual condition; develop a keen eye and ask insightful questions.

- Pray for them regularly.
- Visit or call them.
- Encourage, comfort, counsel, and correct them when needed.
- Warn them of aberrant teachings and worldly influences.
- Feed them on the sustaining bread of life, Holy Scripture.
- Take responsibility for their spiritual welfare.
- Aid them in their daily sanctification.
- Search for them if they wander from the believing community.
- Love them as your own family.

Remember, these sheep are the property of the Good Shepherd, and he cares deeply if any of them are lost. Above all, be an example to the flock.

The People Need You

The flock needs you to do the job that the Holy Spirit has called you to—shepherding God's flock. Do not fail them. Give your life, your time, energy, and best efforts for God's sheep. The Good Shepherd Jesus did that for you! It is the least you can do for him.

Nicolaus Ludwig von Zinzendorf (1700–1760) was born of Austrian nobility and privilege. As a young Christian man traveling throughout Germany, he visited the art museum in Düsseldorf. There he came face-to-face with the famous painting, "Behold the Man" (*Ecce Homo*), by the renowned Italian painter Domenico Feti. It was Pilate who said of the bleeding, thorn-crowned Jesus, "Behold the man!" to the crowd demanding Jesus's death (John 19:5).

As Zinzendorf stood before the painting looking at Christ, positioned before the angry mob beaten and with a crown of thorns upon his head and clothed in a purple robe to mock him, he read these words at the bottom of the painting written in Latin: "This I have suffered for you; now what will you do for me?"

These words deeply moved young Zinzendorf. He realized that, although he was a Christian, and despite being blessed with high position and wealth, he had really done nothing for Christ. So at that time he committed his life to Christ's service. He wrote: "I have loved Him for a long time, but I have never actually done anything for Him. From now on I will do whatever He leads me to do."[18] Zinzendorf became one of the founders of the Moravian movement, wrote over 2,000 hymns, and inspired one of the world's greatest missionary efforts.

My prayer is that, like Zinzendorf, you too may be guided and motivated in your service by beholding Christ's ultimate sacrifice for your salvation: "Consider him who endured from sinners such hostility against himself, so that you may not grow weary or fainthearted" (Heb. 12:3). Give Christ your all!

> You are responsible to watch over all the flock—the whole
> flock, not just your favorites, your friends and
> family, or the people who agree with you.

***All* the Sheep:** Don't miss the little word "all." You are responsible to watch over *all* the flock—the whole flock, not just your favorites, your friends and family, or the people who agree with you. None must be neglected, for all are precious and valuable to God. All are potential meals for the coming wolves. Guard them all, and guard yourself. You also belong to God's flock.

Every-Member Ministry: All this may be overwhelming for you, but remember that you do not complete all these responsibilities alone. You are to shepherd God's flock as a team of biblically qualified, Spirit-appointed elders. Moreover, among the elders some can serve full time, part time, or quarter time at the church's expense. In addition, you have the deacons to assist you in your work.* Furthermore,

---

* See Alexander Strauch, *Paul's Vision for the Deacons: Assisting the Elders with the Care of God's Church* (Littleton, CO: Lewis and Roth, 2017).

in a biblically functioning church, every member is gifted in some way and has a role to play in serving, building up, and caring for the church body. This principle is correctly referred to as "every-member ministry of the body of Christ" (Eph. 4:1–16).

The elders are not to do all the work themselves. Their job is "to equip the saints for the work of ministry, for building up the body of Christ" (Eph. 4:12). These unique Christian truths need to be consistently taught to and modeled for the local church by its shepherd elders.

KEY POINTS TO REMEMBER

1. Your first duty: Be keenly attentive to your own spiritual growth, your relationship with Christ, your moral integrity, and your biblical and theological beliefs.

2. Do not be naïve! Satan has a special eye focused on you. Guard yourself!

3. Create a positive atmosphere among the elders that encourages continuous learning and growth.

4. You are responsible to watch over *all* the flock—not just your favorite ones, friends and family, or the people who agree with you.

---

[1] BDAG, s.v. "προσέχω," 879.
[2] C. K. Barrett, *The Acts of the Apostles*, ICC (T&T Clark, Edinburgh 1998), 974.
[3] Deut. 12:30; Matt. 7:15; 16:6, 12; Mark 13:22–23; Luke 12:1; 20:46; 2 Peter 3:17.
[4] "Beware" translates the same verb (προσέχω) used in Acts 20:28.
[5] A. W. Tozer, *Whatever Happened to Worship?* comp. and ed. Gerald B. Smith (Camp Hill, PA: Christian Publications, 1985), 78.
[6] BDAG, s.v. "ἐπέχω," 362, "to be mindful or especially observant . . . take pains with yourself."
[7] *The NIV Matthew Henry Commentary* (Grand Rapids: Zondervan, 1992), 529.
[8] Richard Baxter, *The Reformed Pastor* (repr. Grand Rapids: Sovereign Grace, 1971), 7.
[9] Ibid, 7.

[10] Paul D. Stanley and J. Robert Clinton, *Connecting: The Mentoring Relationships You Need to Succeed in Life* (Colorado Springs: NavPress, 1992), 222.

[11] Michael Green, *The Second Epistle General of Peter and the General Epistle of Jude*, rev. ed., TNTC (Grand Rapids: Eerdmans, 1987), 163.

[12] Often attributed to Jim Frankel of the Cleveland Press. See Curtis Hutson, *Punch Lines: A Collection of One-liners, Sentence-sermons, and Attention-getters* (Murfreesboro, TN: Sword of the Lord Publishers, 1989), 59.

[13] John Owen, "Of the Mortification of Sin in Believers," chapter 2, in *The Works of John Owen* (Edinburgh: Johnstone and Hunter, 1850–53; repr. Edinburgh: Banner of Truth, 1967), 6:5–86 (esp. 9). This essay was originally written in 1656.

[14] "Letter to the Rev. Dan Edwards," Oct. 2, 1840, in Andrew A. Bonar, *The Life and Remains, Letters, Lectures, and Poems of the Rev. Robert Murray McCheyne* (1844; repr. New York: Robert Carter, 1874), 211. McCheyne wrote,

> How diligently the cavalry officer keeps his sabre clean and sharp; every stain he rubs off with the greatest care. Remember you are God's sword—his instrument—I trust a chosen vessel unto him to bear his name. In great measure, according to the purity and perfections of the instrument, will be the success. It is not great talents God blesses so much as great likeness to Jesus. A holy minister is an awful weapon in the hand of God.

[15] Derek W. H. Thomas, *Acts*, REC (Phillipsburg, NJ: P&R, 2011), 582.

[16] Donald S. Whitney, *Spiritual Disciplines for the Christian Life*, rev. ed. (Colorado Springs: NavPress, 2014). Also recommended is D. A. Carson, *Praying with Paul: A Call to Spiritual Reformation* (Grand Rapids: Baker, 2014).

[17] Jer. 13:17; Zech. 10:3.

[18] https://christianhistoryinstitute.org/magazine/article/the-richyoungruler, accessed October 1, 2020.

CHAPTER 8

Incentives for Guarding God's Church

Pay careful attention to yourselves and to all the flock,
in which the Holy Spirit has made you overseers,
to care for [to shepherd] the church of God,
which he obtained with his own blood.

(Acts 20:28b)

Paul was a skilled motivator. He knew that people need reasons for what they do. So, after his main charge to the elders ("Pay careful attention to yourselves and to all the flock"), he lays out four compelling reasons for why they must guard themselves and all God's flock:

- The Holy Spirit's sovereign will in appointing them as overseers of the church
- The special nature of the Church of God
- The unspeakable price paid to purchase the Church
- The inevitable appearance of sheep-eating wolves, intent on devouring the flock

> You need to know the biblical rationale for devoting
> your life to protecting God's "flock" of people.

If these reasons for guarding yourself and all God's flock are not understood, you will not last long as a church leader. You will not have the right motivation to work hard and endure hardships. The work is too difficult and the problems are overwhelming. Therefore, you need to know the biblical rationale for devoting your life to protecting God's "flock" of people.

THE HOLY SPIRIT'S APPOINTMENT

At his final face-to-face meeting, Paul reminded the elders of this significant fact: It was the Holy Spirit of God who made them "overseers" for the purpose of shepherding God's precious flock: "Pay careful attention to yourselves and to all the flock, in which the Holy Spirit has made you overseers."

The Holy Spirit "made"[1] these elders "overseers" to shepherd God's church. Other Bible translations render the Greek verb as "appointed"[2] or "placed."[3] Whatever English term we use, it was the Spirit's doing! The sovereign Spirit empowered, motivated, and gifted these men to be overseers and shepherds. These elders are overseers by divine placement, initiative, and design.

The Person and Work of the Holy Spirit

Paul stressed the person and work of the Holy Spirit in determining who should shepherd God's people. It was not the church or the apostles that placed these men as overseers. Although human means were not excluded from the process, the placement was ultimately made by a divine Person, God the Holy Spirit. This is a sobering reality; one becomes an overseer by divine appointment. This is an "ordination" greater than any human appointment, as truthfully expressed by the missions writer, Douglas Porter:

Christ, the Son of God, hath sent me
Through the midnight lands;
Mine the mighty ordination
Of the pierced hands.[4]

The Galatian Elders: Earlier in Acts we learn that on their first missionary journey (AD 47), Paul and Barnabas "appointed elders" in every church:

> And when they [Paul and Barnabas] had appointed elders for them in every church, with prayer and fasting they committed them to the Lord in whom they had believed. (Acts 14:23)

In the process of selecting elders, the apostles would have naturally looked for observable evidence that the Holy Spirit was leading and preparing certain ones for the task of shepherding God's flock. (See Paul's list of elder qualifications in 1 Tim. 3:1–7 and Titus 1:5–9.) They would have prayed for the Holy Spirit's guidance for assurance that they were appointing the men of God's choosing. Moreover, the apostles would have consulted the local congregation for corroboration of their choices to provide pastoral leadership for the church. The divine and the human elements work together in this all-important responsibility.

> The only men we should want as overseers of our
> local churches are those in whom the Spirit of God
> has placed the desire, motivation, love, strength,
> and gifting to do the work.

The Influence of the Holy Spirit: Throughout Acts, we see the ever-present influence of the Holy Spirit guiding the apostles in the advancement of the gospel and church planting. One tangible way the Holy Spirit influences and directs local churches is by providing men from within the church itself to oversee and shepherd the flock.

Only Spirit-Appointed Elders: The only men we should want as overseers of our local churches are those in whom the Spirit of God has placed the desire, motivation, love, strength, and gifting to do the work. Since this is God's work, only those whom he has appointed to do his work are qualified.

Do you see yourselves as a Spirit-appointed overseers of God's flock? Or have you been told you are only laymen who serve temporarily? The Holy Spirit appoints spiritual overseers to pastor the flock, not laymen! If you agree that you are a Spirit-appointed overseer, take this responsibility seriously. You are under divine obligation to watch over yourself and God's people with the utmost diligence.

OVERSEERS

Since Paul called for a meeting with "the elders of the church" (v. 17), you might expect him to say that *the Holy Spirit made you elders to shepherd the church of God.* Instead, Paul used the term, *overseers.* "The Holy Spirit has made you overseers." The term *overseers* aptly explains Paul's charge that the elders watch over, guard, and protect God's flock.

The Greek word for *overseer* is *episkopos* (ἐπίσκοπος), which was a well-known, commonly used designation for various kinds of officials. The word conveys the idea of one who watches over, a superintendent, or an official guardian. According to the latest edition of the Bauer-Danker-Arndt-Gingrich *Greek-English Lexicon, episkopos* is:

> One who has the responsibility of safeguarding or seeing to it that something is done in the correct way, guardian. . . .
>
> In the Greco-Roman world *episkopos* frequently refers to one who has a definite function or fixed office of guardianship and related activity within a group. . . . The term was taken over in Christian communities in reference to one who served as *overseer* or *supervisor,* with special interest in guarding the apostolic tradition.[5]

In the following texts, Paul uses the noun *episkopos* as a title to describe local church officials:

> Paul and Timothy, servants of Christ Jesus, to all the saints in Christ Jesus who are at Philippi, with the *overseers* and deacons. (Phil. 1:1)

> If anyone aspires to the office of overseer, he desires a noble task. Therefore an *overseer* must be above reproach. (1 Tim. 3:1–2)

> Appoint elders in every town as I directed you—if anyone is above reproach, the husband of one wife, and his children are believers and not open to the charge of debauchery or insubordination. For *an overseer*, as God's steward, must be above reproach. (Titus 1:5b–7)

Note that Paul refers to an overseer "as God's steward." An overseer is God's household or estate manager, a very important position of trust demanding faithfulness and competancy.

Paul also uses the related noun, *episkopē* (ἐπισκοπή, "oversight," "supervision"), to define the work or position of an overseer:

> The saying is trustworthy: If anyone aspires to the office of overseer (*episkopē*; ἐπισκοπή, overseership), he desires a noble task. Therefore an overseer must be above reproach. (1 Tim. 3:1–2; see Acts 1:20)

Peter uses the verbal form of the word "overseer" to describe the role of the elders:

> So I exhort the elders among you . . . shepherd the flock of God that is among you, exercising oversight [ἐπισκοποῦντες (*episkopountes*), the participial form of ἐπισκοπέω (*episkopeō*)]. (1 Peter 5:1–2)

Here in Acts 20:28, Paul connects the term *overseer* with the elders and their work of shepherding and safeguarding "the church of God."

Character and Function

Overseers and *elders* refer to the same group of governing officers. Paul uses the two terms interchangeably. Although the terms *overseer* and *elder* refer to the same official, they are not exactly synonymous. Each emphasizes different aspects of the office. The term *elder* characterizes spiritual maturity, experience, wisdom, and character. In the Greek translation of the Old Testament, the term *elder* indicated the person was a recognized, mature, community leader.

Both "overseer" and "elder" are needed to capture the full biblical concepts of who and what a biblical elder is to be in character and function.

The term *overseer* stresses the ideas of official oversight, guardianship, and supervision. Both titles are needed to capture the full biblical concepts of who and what a biblical elder is to be in character and function.

Terms Matter

When studying any biblical doctrine, we need to bear in mind that the words and the original meanings of those terms, as used by the sacred writers, matter profoundly for a correct understanding of the writers' thinking and teaching.

It is not by chance that the New Testament writers avoided terms like "priest," "lord," "ruler," and "king" when describing local church officials. These terms do not fit the unique family nature of the Christian brotherhood and sisterhood, or the amazing realities of the Spirit-indwelt body of Christ, with all of its various gifts and functions.

Significantly, the New Testament writers did not emphasize lofty or sacred titles for local church leaders. That occurred much later in the centuries to follow, when church leaders became obsessed with titles and positions of power.

Different denominations use various terms to describe their leaders: "pastor," "minister," "preacher," "rector," "bishop," "elder," "deacon," or "priest." Here in this biblical study of Paul's Miletus address to the Ephesian elders, *we will stay with the New Testament's own terminology and concepts for describing those in the official leadership role of the local church.*

A Pastoral Team of Overseers

As the word itself indicates, "overseers" are officially responsible for the overall supervision, protection, and care of God's "flock" of people. But do not fail to recognize that Paul did not call for the "overseer" of the church, nor the "senior pastor," nor the "bishop" over the churches. Paul was not addressing a professional, ordained clergy. He called for the "elders of the church." Most of these men were probably self-supported after Paul's example (Acts 20:34–35), with a few elders financially supported by the church body (1 Tim. 5:17–18; Gal. 6:6).

Plurality: Acts 20 substantiates the biblical pattern of elders having pastoral oversight over the local church by jointly shepherding as "a pastoral team." John Stott—a former Anglican rector of All Souls Church in London, and a highly respected biblical commentator—challenges us to recover this biblical concept of "a pastoral team." Note that Stott has allowed the biblical evidence to shape his thinking rather than traditional clericalism:

> There is no biblical warrant either for the one-man-band (a single pastor playing all the instruments of the orchestra himself) or for a hierarchical or pyramidal structure

in the local church (a single pastor perched at the apex of a pyramid). It is not even clear that each of the elders was in charge of an individual house-church. It is better to think of them as a team, some perhaps with the oversight of house-churches, but others with specialist ministries according to their gifts, and all sharing the pastoral care of Christ's flock. We need today to recover this concept of a pastoral team in the church.[6]

Always keep in mind this undeniable truth: Our Lord himself appointed the first leadership body over his Church. Jesus gave us the plurality of leaders in the twelve apostles—not one senior apostle accompanied by eleven assistants, but twelve apostles working together in unity to lead and teach the first Christian church. (For the important concept of first among equals, see www.Acts20book.com.)

> Our Lord himself appointed the first leadership body over his Church. Jesus gave us the plurality of leaders in the twelve apostles—not one senior apostle accompanied by eleven assistants, but twelve apostles working together in unity to lead and teach the first Church.

More Eyes and More Ears: One very practical reason for the plurality of elders is for better protection of the local church from "fierce wolves." In light of Paul's chilling predictions of false teachers from both outside and inside the church, having multiple overseers will provide more eyes and ears for seeing and dealing with this threat. Besides, multiple overseers can provide better mutual support and encouragement as they battle "against the spiritual forces of evil in the heavenly places" (Eph. 6:12).[7]

Not all elders are equally equipped to detect the subtleties of false teaching. Therefore, in this particular aspect of shepherding, *some will contribute more to the eldership through their gifting in theological and biblical discernment.* As Paul put it: "The members do not all have the same function ... Having gifts that differ according to the grace given to us" (Rom. 12:4, 6). "Now there are varieties of gifts ... varieties of activities, but it is the same God who empowers them all in everyone" (1 Cor. 12:4–6). "But as it is, God arranged the members in the body, each one of them, as he chose" (1 Cor. 12:18). *Each elder will have his own gifts and special contribution to make to the whole leadership team.*

In light of Paul's chilling predictions of false teachers from both outside and inside the church, having multiple overseers will provide more eyes and ears for seeing and dealing with this threat.

SHEPHERD THE CHURCH OF GOD

The Holy Spirit has placed overseers in the flock for this express purpose: "to care for the church of God" (Acts 20:28). The *English Standard Version*'s translation of the Greek text is disappointing. It reads, "to care for the church of God." However, the Greek verb rendered "care for" is the Greek verb for *shepherd* (ποιμαίνω [*poimainō*]).[8] Literally the text reads, "to shepherd the church of God."

The verb *shepherd* is much richer, more vivid than the general term "care for." Of course, the idea of caring for people would be included in the shepherd-flock image. Since the local church is called "a flock"[9] it needs to have shepherds and to be shepherded. The Holy Spirit appointed the elders *for this purpose*—to shepherd the church of God.

Peter and the Shepherd Elders

Like Paul, Peter directly addressed the church elders, but by letter. Like Paul, Peter also used the shepherd-flock motif to exhort the elders to do their work: "So I exhort the elders among you . . . shepherd the flock of God that is among you, exercising oversight" (1 Peter 5:1–2).

> Since the two preeminent apostles charged
> the elders—and no other person or group—to
> shepherd God's flock, we can conclude that, in biblical
> terms, the elders are responsible for the pastoral
> oversight of the local church.

Peter uses terms similar to Paul's in the Miletus speech: *flock, shepherd* (verb), *overseers/oversight*. These two passages should always be studied together when considering the identity and work of the New Testament elders.[10]

Since the two preeminent apostles charged the elders—and no other person or group—to shepherd God's flock, we can conclude that, in biblical terms, the elders are responsible for the pastoral oversight of the local church.

Spiritually Gifted Shepherds

In Ephesians 4:11 Paul used the noun *shepherd* to describe a spiritually gifted person: "And he gave the apostles, the prophets, the evangelists, the shepherds and teachers, to equip the saints for the work of ministry." This is the only New Testament passage in which the noun *shepherd* is specifically used of a church leader.[11] The shepherd gift entails both leading and teaching.[12] We should not expect that every elder has been given the specific gift of shepherd. However, no matter what spiritual gifts each of the individual members have, the church eldership is to be the shepherding body of the local church. A Spirit-gifted shepherd would be an exceedingly valuable person to the local church and to the eldership body itself.

The purpose for giving the evangelists, shepherds, and teachers is for them to equip/prepare the saints for the work of ministry in order to build up the body of Christ (Eph. 4:12). We dare not miss the significance of this passage of Scripture.

The Shepherding Task

The biblical imagery of shepherding perfectly matches the Holy Spirit's design for the overseeing elders. The Greek verb "to shepherd" explains in a more comprehensive way what the elders are expected to do. To literally shepherd a flock involves various skills and tasks:

- Leading sheep out from the fold daily to pastureland and water
- Providing them time to rest
- Protecting them from wild beasts, human thieves, tormenting insects, or weather
- Finding straying or lost sheep
- Gathering scattered sheep into the fold at night
- Shearing
- Lambing
- Doctoring their health needs
- Being prepared to meet the various needs of the flock as they present themselves.

Like literal shepherds, *shepherd elders must be fully invested in the comprehensive work of shepherding God's people.* They are not "board elders," sitting in a meeting once a month making decisions.

In the context of the Acts 20 discourse, the protecting aspect of the shepherding task is stressed the most. The flock must be protected from the ever-present danger of savage wolves. This necessitates courageous shepherd elders who are alert to false teachers.

Shepherd elders must be fully invested in the comprehensive work of shepherding God's people.

Study the Imagery of Shepherding

Many of us today lack a correct mental image of literal shepherds in ancient, biblical times. D. A. Carson makes this same point:

> Many people in the industrialized West (though not Australians!) are inclined to think of shepherds as sentimental beings, perhaps somewhat effeminate, with their arms full of cuddly lambs, and the English adjective 'good' does nothing to dissuade us from these misconceptions. But the shepherd's job was tiring, manly and sometimes dangerous.[13]

If you are unfamiliar with this imagery, I recommend that you study this God-given metaphor for explaining the work of biblical leaders. The more you know about the shepherd-sheep relationship, the more you will better understand the responsible task God has called you to do.

A good start on a study of shepherds and sheep is Phillip Keller's book, *A Shepherd Looks at Psalm 23*.[14] For me, learning about the work of shepherding sheep has been, and still is, enjoyable and educational.

The time-honored sheep-shepherd image is still relevant today because people are like sheep. And the work of spiritual leadership is basically the same as tending sheep—feeding, leading, and protecting the believing community. In brief, the imagery of shepherding a flock communicates the following concepts.

Hard Work: Shepherding is hard work. Those who are "allergic" to work will not be good church shepherds.

Long Hours: A shepherd's work is never done. It starts early in the morning by leading the sheep out of the fold to fresh pasture and water, being with them all day, returning them to the fold in the evening, and guarding them at night. There may also be late night deliveries of the newborn or feedings of the lambs (Gen. 31:39–40).

Sacrifice: Shepherding requires much self-sacrifice on the part of the shepherd, as he must put the needs of the flock before his own.

Dangerous Work: The shepherd must be alert to danger and vigilant at all times. Sheep must be protected from wild beasts (like the wolf, lion, leopard, or bear). This means that the shepherd must also have courage like David who rescued sheep from the mouths of lions and bears (1 Sam. 17:34–37). He must even be watchful for men who would steal his sheep.

Skill and Knowledge: Shepherding is not for dummies. It requires a great deal of knowledge and many different kinds of skills, especially proficiency in the skill of feeding the flock properly.

> You cannot be an absentee elder or an invisible elder and expect to be a good shepherd. Your consistent presence with the sheep is necessary to your work of shepherding.

Presence: One of the most intriguing aspects of shepherding is the shepherd's personal presence among the sheep. The shepherd-flock motif is *a highly relational one, showing personalized care.* The shepherd and the flock form a close bond together. The sheep know the shepherd's voice, and he knows his sheep by name.

You cannot be an absentee elder or an invisible elder and expect to be a good shepherd. Your consistent presence with the sheep is necessary to your work of shepherding.

Love: Ultimately, the shepherd must love the sheep if he is to succeed in tenderly caring for them. In Spain, I sat with a shepherd in a field for a long while, asking him questions about being a shepherd and caring for sheep. At the end of our conversation, I asked him, "What's the most important thing about being a shepherd?" He responded, "You must love sheep."

Authority: The shepherd has authority over the sheep, to lead them and to correct them. He has been entrusted with this authority and is answerable to the flock's owner for the flock's health and safety.

Contemporary Application

Shepherd imagery beautifully blends the concepts of authority and leadership with self-sacrifice, tenderness, loving care, and intimate relationships.

To shepherd God's people means to:

- Feed the people the life-giving sustenance of God's Word
- Provide competent leadership for making
  sound decisions for the congregation
- Address difficulties and problems
- Protect the church from infighting and false doctrines
- Grow the flock
- Seek out lost members
- Pray for the sheep
- Visit, counsel, marry, and bury them

There is no reason for you to be confused about your role as church elders. You are to be spiritual shepherds, jointly protecting, teaching, leading, and practically caring for God's people.

THE NATURE OF THE FLOCK: THE CHURCH OF GOD

The elders shepherd no ordinary group of people; it is "the church of God" they lead. The "church of God" was earlier called by the metaphor "the flock." The word "church" here designates the local congregation/assembly of redeemed people in Ephesus. The phrase "church of God" is commonly used by Paul.[15] "Paul in particular," writes Eckhard J. Schnabel, "emphasizes that the ἐκκλησία [ekklēsía] belongs to God."[16] He goes on to say:

The genitive "of God" describes God as the initiator and owner of the congregation of believers in Jesus—the company of followers of Jesus has been established by God (genitive of authorship) and thus belongs to God (possessive genitive).[17]

The local church does not belong to the elders, the apostles, or any other person or group. It does not belong to Martin Luther, John Calvin, or John Wesley, or any other individual or denomination. It is "the church of God, which he obtained with his own blood." God called this company of people into existence. He is the one who sustains it, provides for it, and cares for it. Biblical commentator Andreas Köstenberger points out that the phrase "'God's church' underscores the sacredness and solemn responsibility of caring for God's people."[18]

> Don't be a passive shepherd, don't be an invisible
> elder, and don't be a spectator.

Throughout this entire speech to "the elders of the church," Paul has been concerned for the education, protection, and care of the "church of God" in Ephesus. In Paul's absence, the eldership team must now teach, evangelize, protect, and care for God's church. They must love the church of God as Paul does because it was purchased with the precious blood of his own Son.

It is the congregation of the redeemed that the Holy Spirit has assigned you to oversee and shepherd. As Christ's undershepherds, you have a very important task to perform—don't be a passive shepherd, don't be an invisible elder, and don't be a spectator.

The Immense Value of the Church of God

Paul next expresses the magnitude of the worth of the Church of God with this fact: "which he obtained with his own blood." In the concise words of David Gooding, former professor of Greek at Queen's

University, Belfast, Ireland: "With this we touch the mainspring of all true defense and shepherding of the church: the cost at which God bought it."[19]

Bible translators struggle over both the correct Greek text and the proper translation of this clause.[20] But we need not permit these technical problems to detract from the statement's intent and powerful impact. Whether we translate the phrase as "his [God's] own blood," or "the blood of his own one [Jesus Christ]" (which is preferred here), *the point regarding the immeasurable worth of God's congregation of people is still made.*

> "With this we touch the mainspring of all true defense and shepherding of the church: the cost at which God bought it." —David Gooding

God acquired[21] this group of people by means of the shed blood of his one and only Son, Jesus Christ. By *blood* Paul meant death. More specifically, he meant shed blood or sacrificial death, that is, the life violently taken from Christ at the cross, as the Old Testament system of sacrifice demonstrates. At the core of the Christian faith lies the penal, substitutionary atonement of Christ upon the cross. Succinctly put, "Christ, our Passover lamb, has been sacrificed" (1 Cor. 5:7).[22]

Jesus was God's lamb, given as a willing, sinless, once-for-all sacrifice for sin. Isaiah prophesied of the suffering servant, Jesus: "He was pierced for our transgressions; he was crushed for our iniquities. . . . Like a lamb that is led to the slaughter . . . so he opened not his mouth" (Isa. 53:5, 7).

"By his blood" is the glorious theme of the heavenly angelic choir surrounding the exalted Lord Jesus Christ:

> "Worthy are you to take the scroll . . . for you were slain, and *by your blood you ransomed people for God* from every tribe and language and people and nation." (Rev. 5:9)

Or as the writer to the Hebrews puts it: "[Jesus] did not enter by means of the blood of goats and calves; but he entered the Most Holy Place once for all *by his own blood*, having obtained eternal redemption" (Heb. 9:12; NIV). The writer of Hebrews goes on to say: "without the shedding of blood there is no forgiveness of sins" (Heb. 9:22).

Never forget the price paid!

The unforgettable words, "the blood of his own one," should come to mind whenever you are serving the Lord's people. Even when you are discouraged by their behavior, or you want to quit, remember that they were acquired by God by means of the blood of his only Son, Jesus. Never forget the price paid!

The Incalculable Price Paid

The sum one is willing to pay for an object speaks to its value. For the Church, God gave his one and only Son as a sin-bearing sacrifice to atone for our sin. How could God have paid more for his people? He paid an incalculable price. How he must love the Church!

It means a great deal to God when we earnestly lead and protect his blood-bought children. Richard Baxter dramatically captures the passion of Paul's persuasive reasoning:

> Can you not hear [Christ] saying, "Did I die for these people, and will you then refuse to look after them? Were they worth My blood, and are they not worth your labor? Did I come down from Heaven to seek and to save that which was lost, and will you refuse to go next door, or to the next street or village to seek them? How small is your labor or condescension compared to Mine! I debased Myself to do this, but it is your honor to be so employed. Have I done and suffered so much for their salvation, and will you refuse that little that lies upon your hands?"[23]

Every time you look out on the congregation, say this to yourself: *These people were purchased by the precious blood of the Lord Jesus Christ. I should regard them as most valuable to God.* What an immense honor it is then to love and shepherd God's people!

The Trinity

Another matter to observe in this passage is that Paul refers to all three members of the Godhead. God the Father acquires the Church by means of his Son, who, in submission to the Father, gives his life for the redemption of sinners, and the Holy Spirit guides Paul and places overseers in the local church to shepherd God's sheep.

Throughout Paul's challenge, God, Christ, and the Holy Spirit have been at the center of Paul's message:

- "Serving the Lord [Jesus] with all humility" (v. 19)
- "Repentance toward God" (v. 21)
- "Faith in our Lord Jesus Christ" (v. 21)
- "Constrained by the Spirit" (v. 22)
- "The Holy Spirit testifies to me" (v. 23)
- "The ministry that I received from the Lord Jesus" (v. 24)
- "The gospel of the grace of God" (v. 24)
- "The whole counsel of God" (v. 27)
- "The Holy Spirit has made you overseers" (v. 28)
- "The church of God" (v. 28)
- "The blood of his own one [Jesus]" (v. 28)
- "I commend you to God" (v. 32)
- "To the word of his [God's] grace" (v. 32)
- "The words of the Lord Jesus" (v. 35)

The gospel and the Church are the creation of the triune God of the Bible, and you have been called to protect his gospel and his people with your life. Do not fail the Lord and his people.

KEY POINTS TO REMEMBER

1. Know the biblical rationale for why you should devote your life to guarding God's "flock" from false teachers.

2. The only men you should want as elders are those in whom the Holy Spirit has placed the desire, motivation, love, strength, and gifting to do the work.

3. The elders, that is, the overseers, are responsible to pastor the church of God.

4. Shepherd imagery beautifully blends the concepts of authority and leadership with self-sacrifice, tenderness, loving care, and intimate relationship.

5. Ponder the magnitude of the worth of the church of God and the inestimable price paid to obtain her, which is, the precious blood of the Son of God.

6. You have been called by the Spirit to protect his gospel and his people with your life.

---

[1] BDAG, s.v. "τίθημι," "to cause to undergo a change in experience/condition, make, consign," 1004. The NIV; NRSV; NASB; NKJV; NLT all translate the verb here as "made."

[2] "Appointed," CSB; Eckhard J. Schnabel, *Acts*, ZECNT (Grand Rapids: Zondervan, 2012), 846; *NIDNTTE*, "τίθημι," 4:491; see 1 Cor. 12:28; 1 Tim. 1:12; 2:7; 2 Tim. 1:11.

[3] "Placed in your care," GNB.

[4] Douglas D. Porter, *At Thy Disposal. The Beginnings of the Egypt General Mission* (London: Egypt Mission, 1934), 2. Quoted by Klaus Fiedler, *The Story of Faith Missions: From Hudson Taylor to Present Day Africa* (Oxford: Regnum Books, 1994), 187.

[5] BDAG, s.v. "ἐπίσκοπος," 379.

[6] John Stott, *The Spirit, the Church, and the World: The Message of Acts* (Downers Grove, IL: InterVarsity, 1990), 324. To better understand equality and diversity within the eldership, see the article *First Among Equals*, available on www.LewisandRoth.org > Downloads > Helpful Links.

[7] For further reasons for the plurality of elders, see Alexander Strauch, *Biblical Eldership: An Urgent Call to Restore Biblical Church Leadership* (Littleton, CO: Lewis and Roth, 1995), 35–50.

[8] "Shepherd," CSB, NASB, NKJV, NRSV; "Be shepherds," NIV, GNB; "Feed and shepherd," NLT; "the Holy Spirit has given you charge, as shepherds," REB.

[9] The noun ποίμνιον (*poimnion*).

[10] Some 30 years before Peter wrote his letter, Jesus directly charged him to shepherd his sheep (John 21:15–17). The shepherd-sheep motif goes back to Jesus himself. He said, "I am the good shepherd " (John 10:11), and he called us his "sheep." He also said, "The good shepherd lays down his life for the sheep."

[11] "It is best to translate this as 'shepherds', so retaining the original underlying image and avoiding all the overtones in the modern use of 'pastor'" (Ernest Best, *Ephesians*, ICC [Edinburgh: T&T Clark, 1998], 392).

[12] See Daniel B. Wallace, *Greek Grammar: Beyond the Basics* (Grand Rapids: Zondervan, 1996), 284.

[13] D. A. Carson, *The Gospel According to John* (Grand Rapids: Eerdmans, 1991), 385–386.

[14] See Phillip Keller, *A Shepherd Looks at Psalm 23* (Grand Rapids: Zondervan, 2007). He also has an excellent book on John 10 titled *A Shepherd Looks at the Good Shepherd*, which I highly recommend.

[15] Acts 20:28; 1 Cor. 1:2; 10:32; 11:16 (plural), 22; 15:9; 2 Cor. 1:1; Gal. 1:13; 1 Thess. 2:14 (plural); 2 Thess. 1:4 (plural); 1 Tim. 3:5, 15.

[16] Eckhard J. Schnabel, *Acts*, ECNT (Grand Rapids: Zondervan, 2012), 289, note 25.

[17] Schnabel, *Acts*, 289.

[18] Andreas Köstenberger, *Commentary on 1–2 Timothy & Titus*, Biblical Theology for Christian Proclamation (Nashville, TN: B&H, 2017), 130.

[19] David Gooding, *True to the Faith, The Acts of the Apostles: Defining and Defending the Gospel* (Coleraine, N. Ireland: Myrtlefield Trust, 2013), 426.

[20] The best rendering seems to be, "the church of God, which He obtained by means of the blood of his [God's] own one." His own one is Jesus.

[21] L&N, s.v. "περιποιέομαι," 1:565, "to acquire possession of something, with the probable component of considerable effort—'to acquire, to achieve, to win.' . . . 'be shepherds of the church of God, which he acquired by means of his own Son's death.'"

[22] Alan M. Stibbs, *The Meaning of the Word "Blood" in Scripture*, 2nd ed. (London: Tyndale, 1954), 1–32; Leon Morris, *The Apostolic Preaching of the Cross*, 3rd ed. (London: Tyndale, 1965), 126–128.

[23] Richard Baxter, *The Reformed Pastor*, (repr. Grand Rapids: Sovereign Grace, 1971), 55.

CHAPTER 9

Fierce Wolves Are Coming; Be Alert

I know that after my departure fierce wolves will come in among you, not sparing the flock; and from among your own selves will arise men speaking twisted things, to draw away the disciples after them. Therefore be alert, remembering that for three years I did not cease night or day to admonish every one with tears.

(Acts 20:29–31)

Weighing heavily on Paul's heart was the imminent danger his dear friends would soon face after his departure. He knew the enemy so well that he could say with certainty: "I know . . . fierce wolves will come in among you." He didn't say, "I think," "possibly," "maybe," or "who knows?" He said, "I know."

There was no doubt in his mind; this was going to happen. Like all capable leaders, *Paul was a man with foresight.* He was not naïve to the cruel realities of a world at war with its Creator. He had personally experienced many dangers and attacks by the enemies of the cross of Christ.

Note that Paul didn't promise the elders that things would get better over time, or that their best days were ahead, or that they need not be overly concerned. On the contrary, his warnings were meant to shake and wake any elder who might be complacent or naïve to the dangers ahead.

Since the beginning of time, false teachers and prophets have tried to deceive God's people from believing the truth of God's Word. The Old Testament Scriptures warned about fake prophets, corrupt priests, idolatrous kings, and failed elders. We should never be surprised by false teachers, who are in reality *agents of Satan*.

Every new generation has to face its own fierce wolves. That's the way it has always been, and is, and will always be till the Lord comes. What Paul was doing here was preparing the elders for future attacks by cunning predators who intend to devour God's flock and distort the truths of the gospel.

THE ARCHENEMY OF THE CHURCH OF JESUS CHRIST

Modern armies and their military planners often speak of military preparedness. If an enemy nation attempts to attack an advanced nation, the military forces of that nation would be ready to respond in minutes, not days. Planes would be in the air in minutes, not hours. Preparedness is a major deterrent to an enemy.

It has been pointed out that: "By failing to prepare, you are preparing to fail."[1] *Paul did not fail to prepare the church and its presbyters for the inevitable attacks of the archenemies of the Church of Jesus Christ.* Preparedness was a chief concern of Paul's.

Wolves from Without

Following Paul's main charge for the elders to pay strict attention to themselves and all the flock, he bolstered his exhortation with the ominous prediction that "fierce wolves" were coming to devour the flock. Verses 29–30 explain the reason they need to pay careful attention to themselves and to all the flock.

Since the local church is figuratively called a "flock," logically its enemies are figuratively called "wolves," the proverbial predators of sheep and goats. These intruders are like a pack of ravenous wolves intent on devouring the sheep—as Paul puts it, "Not sparing the flock." Wolves are strong and cunning hunters; they have bravado. They are persistent and seem to have boundless energy. They attack from every angle. They are violent. They are insatiable and merciless if allowed to infiltrate the flock.

Government Persecutors: Paul does not specifically say who these wolves from without are. He refers to them as fierce wolves, who are from outside the flock, and who will not spare the flock from destruction. These wolves were not Christian believers. They were seeking to destroy God's people. These wolves from without may have been government officials who despised the Christian faith and fiercely persecuted Christians, many of whom converted from the pagan religion of Rome.

The Romans were polytheists who proudly prized their many ancient gods and splendid culture. They looked down on the God of the Jews and Christians, and saw Christians as a threat to the Roman way of life and religion. Christians wanted to convert people to the new religion, which meant turning away from the beliefs and gods of the Roman Empire. This had to be stopped!

The Judaizers: It is also possible that these fierce wolves could refer to the Judaizers who would infiltrate Paul's churches soon after his departure. They taught a works-based, Torah-keeping gospel message. They sought converts from Paul's churches. For example, Luke records that, while Paul and Barnabas were teaching in the church at Antioch,

> some men came down from Judea and were teaching the brothers, "Unless you are circumcised according to the custom of Moses, you cannot be saved." And after Paul and Barnabas had

no small dissension and debate with them, Paul and Barnabas and some of the others were appointed to go up to Jerusalem to the apostles and the elders about this question. (Acts 15:1–2)

As courageous defenders of the faith, Paul and Barnabas "had no small dissension and debate with them." Paul and Barnabas are good models of competent leaders who were alert, acting immediately in the defense of the gospel and the protection of the church of God. They were not weak leaders. They firmly resisted the advancements of these itinerant Judaizing teachers. *They demonstrate what shepherd elders are to do in such cases, take immediate action!*

> Titanic secular pressure is forcing Christian believers and churches to conform to its standards of morality, sexuality, gender identity, marriage, truth, and secularized religion.

Secularists: Most relevant to Bible-believing Christians today is the inescapable, ubiquitous influence of secular philosophy and worldly values upon the local church. The fierce wolves of secularism are infiltrating our churches and homes aided by the internet, social media, TV, movies, advertising, schools, books, and even some Christian preachers.

Titanic secular pressure is forcing many Christian believers and churches to conform to its standards of morality, sexuality, gender identity, marriage, truth, and secularized religion. Like the proverbial frog in the kettle, some Christians have already become desensitized to the rising heat of secular dogma.

What Paul wrote to the early Christians in the sophisticated city of Rome needs to be repeated loudly and frequently today: "Do not be conformed to this world" (Rom. 12:2). In his translation of the New Testament, J. B. Phillips makes this well-known paraphrase of Romans 12:2: "Don't let the world around you squeeze you into its own mold."[2] Of the worldly church in Corinth, it has been astutely observed: "The problem was not that the church was in Corinth but that too much of Corinth was in the church."[3] Likewise, we need to be keenly aware that we are in the world as God's witnesses, but not of the world's cultural value system.

> "Don't let the world around you squeeze you into
> its own mold." —J. B. Phillips

False Teachers from Within the Church

Even more subtle and frightening than wolves from outside the flock, is that "from among your own selves will arise men speaking twisted things, to draw away the disciples after them" (v. 30). Prophetically, the apostle warns the elders to expect this frightening reality: False teachers will arise even from within the believing community, or from within the eldership itself!

Scripture Twisters: These wolfish shepherds speak "twisted things" (v. 30), distorting and perverting apostolic, orthodox doctrine. They tie the true teachings of Scripture into false, complex knots that even confuse learned scholars. They are slippery creatures who cannot be easily pinned down; they are experts at double-talk and diversion. You cannot have an honest discussion with them because they lack intellectual honesty. Masters of subtlety and novelty, false teachers mix truth with error, and confuse people with half-truths and complex ideas. Like Satan confronting Jesus in the wilderness, they can quote the Scriptures with great ease. They have a way of wearing people down with their arguments so that most people capitulate, weary of trying to argue.

Sheep Stealers: These apostate teachers also want their own disciples, so they seek "to draw away the disciples after them" (v. 30). A disciple is a follower of a distinguished teacher or master, a pupil, student, and learner. All Christian believers are disciples of Jesus Christ. These pseudo-Christian teachers want to draw disciples away from Christ, our supreme teacher (Matt. 23:8), and his chosen apostles in order to garner their own followers.

Inevitably, these false teachers establish subgroups within the church. They are prepared to fight for their views and to aggressively challenge or silence any opposition. *They are intimidators*; they don't back down from their beliefs, and can argue for hours with anyone who tries to reason with them. I know from personal experience how frustrating it is to argue with such people over doctrine. They care nothing for the church's unity or safety; they care only for themselves and their warped and twisted ideas. They cannot be reasoned with in any sensible way.

Paul's Prophecy Fulfilled: Several years after Paul's meeting at Miletus, this very thing happened in the church at Ephesus. Men like Hymenaeus, Alexander, and Philetus arose from within the church speaking "twisted things."[4] These men were professing believers and church teachers (maybe even elders), but self-deceived: "Desiring to be teachers of the law, without understanding either what they are saying or the things about which they make confident assertions" (1 Tim. 1:7).

Hymenaeus and Philetus were teaching that the bodily resurrection "[had] already happened." These men, Paul wrote Timothy, had "swerved from the truth" (2 Tim. 2:18). Their teachings, he warned, "will spread like gangrene" (v. 17) throughout the church if not stopped. They were already "upsetting the faith of some" (v. 18), so immediate action was necessary to stop the spread of gangrene in the church body at Ephesus.

To halt the dangerous infection of false teaching in the church, Paul sent Timothy to Ephesus to stop the false teachers from spreading their poisonous doctrines (1 Tim. 1:3). False teachers are the archenemies of the Church of Jesus Christ. Their presence can only bring chaos and division.

A Secularized Christ and a Perverse Gospel: Today millions of people worldwide profess to be Christians but follow the secularized gospel and false Christ of liberal theologians and pastors who have thoroughly revised historic, biblical Christianity to mirror secular philosophy. In his book, *Christianity and Liberalism*, J. Gresham Machan rightly judged that liberal Protestantism is a totally different religion from historical, orthodox, biblical Christianty.[5] It preaches a Christ and gospel that atheists, agnostics, and secularists can find agreeable.

The advocates of this reframed Christian religion deny the deity of Christ, and reject the triune nature of God, the divine inspiration and binding authority of Scripture, and the existence of the devil. They discard miracles, the virgin birth, the bodily resurrection, and the first eleven chapters of Genesis, claiming that portion of Scripture to be ancient myth. They fiercely oppose original sin; substitutionary atonement; justification by faith alone; and eternal judgment. Some even deny there is a personal God, certainly not the God presented in Holy Scripture.

These deceivers preach a cross-less, inoffensive gospel of "love," tolerance, and social justice. They present Jesus as the mild-mannered humanist who accepts everyone and deserves our respect only as a "Great Teacher." These learned scholars are masters at taking biblical statements and words and completely redefining them to mean something radically different from what Scripture originally meant. They boldly claim to be the "true teachers" of modernized Christianity, "saving" the gospel from teachings that are "out-of-date" according to modern sensitivities and the scientific age. They are wolves in shepherd's clothes.

Satan's Agents

The advocates of secular Christianity may appear attractive and have charismatic personalities, great intelligence, prominence, and advanced degrees from the most prestigious seminaries and universities. They may have authored popular books presenting exciting, new theological ideas about God and Christ. But Paul calls them out for who they really are, and he minces no words in his description:

> For such men are false apostles, deceitful workmen, disguising themselves as apostles of Christ. And no wonder, for even Satan disguises himself as an angel of light. So it is no surprise if his servants, also, disguise themselves as servants of righteousness. (2 Cor. 11:13–15)

Paul's actual presence was a powerful deterrent against those masquerading as servants of Christ. He fought tirelessly against the infiltration of itinerant false teachers into his churches. Paul's whole life was spent "in the defense and confirmation of the gospel" (Phil. 1:7). When it came to the truth of the gospel, Paul would "not yield in submission even for a moment" (Gal. 2:5). His most scathing anathema fell on those who attempted to add to Christ's gospel:

> There are some who trouble you and want to distort the gospel of Christ. But even if we or an angel from heaven should preach to you a gospel contrary to the one we preached you, let him be accursed. (Gal. 1:7–8)

For three years in Ephesus, Paul had thoroughly proclaimed and defended the gospel. But his departure marked a crucial moment in the life of the Ephesian church. Now that he was leaving, *it was the Ephesian elders' duty to detect and fight off wolves in sheep's clothing.* They could not be naïve. False Christs and false gospels were and are a never-ending reality on this sin-cursed planet. Jesus promised it; his word is sure (Matt. 24:5; Mark 13:6).

> False Christs and false gospels were and are
> a never-ending reality on this sin-cursed planet.

148

Discerning Shepherds

You can now see the critical need for discerning shepherds, who will stand their ground for gospel truth with courage and determination. Churches without discerning shepherds are easy pickings for hungry wolves, who are naturally intuitive hunters, picking out the weak or the young in a flock. The same is true of false teachers. They naturally zero in on weak churches and their leaders. Biblically malnourished churches are an easy meal for hungry predators.

Legitimate Disagreements: To be perfectly clear, I'm not referring to legitimate disagreements among Bible-believing Christians over nonessential doctrines. There will always be doctrinal differences among true believers. The trouble is that there are misguided, unbalanced Christians who label anyone who disagrees with them and their beliefs as false teachers or wolves. Wolves are not true believers. This mentality hurts the body of Christ because it leads to endless divisions and sects among true believers who should love one another despite their differences. Some of the darkest moments in church history show Christians killed by other Christians over issues of baptism, the Lord's Supper, and church discipline.

In fact, judging every disagreement to be heresy actually diminishes the reality of true heresy. If the cry "Wolf!" rings out too often, eventually no one listens, even when the warning is real and the predator is at the gate.

BE ALERT AND BE READY TO ACT

In light of imminent danger, Paul concludes, "Therefore be alert" (v. 31). The Greek verb "alert" literally means "to stay awake," "not sleep." It is often used figuratively in the New Testament, meaning "to be in constant readiness, be on the alert."[6] In other words, "be vigilant."

The verb is a present tense, imperative verb of command: "keep on being alert, be constantly watchful." The term describes a mental and spiritual attitude of vigilance and preparedness. The opposite is to be oblivious to danger, not conscious of the reality of predators, mentally asleep, and preoccupied with activities other than those required of the shepherd watchman at the time.

You cannot guard yourself or God's flock if your eyes are not wide open, your ears alert, and your brain engaged to detect potential perils. Shepherds simply cannot be sleep-walking and alert at the same time.

This is the second of Paul's two principal, imperative commands: "Pay careful attention" (προσέχω [prosechō]) and "be alert" (γρηγορέω [grēgoreō]).

Paul directly charges the elders to be spiritually alert, wide awake, fully alive, and fully engaged in the work of guarding God's people.

Pastoral Alertness

The verb "alert" fits the pastoral imagery of Paul's exhortation. A good shepherd is always conscious of, and alert to, hungry predators. A good watchman is always conscious of and alert to invading armies or thieves by night. A good shepherd elder is always conscious of and alert to false teachers and their heretical teachings. "Unceasing vigilance is the essential requirement in shepherds," writes David Gooding.[7]

Paul knew all too well the human tendency to be oblivious to much of what is going on around them or in the world, to be preoccupied with the wrong things; to be passive; to be minimalists; to be lazy, to want the title but not the work. Therefore, Paul directly charges the elders to be spiritually alert, wide awake, fully alive, and fully engaged in the work of guarding God's people.

Watchfulness: All Christians are urged to "be watchful" (1 Cor. 16:13), but this must be doubly true for church leaders, since they watch over the souls of other people. Sleepy elders produce sleepy churches. Such churches are not alert to the hungry lion, "the devil," who is relentlessly on the prowl for his next meal (1 Peter 5:8).

PAUL'S PERSONAL EXAMPLE OF ALERTNESS

To strengthen his urgent call to be alert, Paul cited his own example: "Remembering that for three years I did not cease night and day to admonish every one with tears" (v. 31). Paul's life is a case study of pastoral vigilance in action. The greater portion of Paul's speech to the elders is a rehearsal and defense of his personal example while he taught at Ephesus:

> Paul's address to the Ephesian elders is remarkable for this, that his exhortation to defend the church of God occupies scarcely more than four verses; but the model he offers of how the defense should be conducted occupies at least thirteen. The model he offers is of course himself and his behavior towards the church during the years he was with them.[8]

Paul is the biblical role model of sound pastoral vigilance for all serious, spiritually-minded church leaders. He shows us how it should be done.

Ceaseless Admonition

Paul's efforts entailed consistently admonishing the believers about wolves in sheep's clothing. The Greek verb for "admonish" means "to warn," "advise," or "instruct."[9] To admonish is to exert a corrective influence in a positive, caring way:

The basic idea is that of the well-meaning earnestness with which one seeks to influence the mind and disposition by appropriate instruction, exhortation, warning and correction.[10]

In the present context, admonishing involves warning believers about the subtle, ongoing dangers of false teachers and the all-too-common human tendency to become inattentive.

Paul's admonitions started when he first arrived in Ephesus. He didn't wait until his departure to warn the people about inevitable confrontations with gospel deniers. He admonished them "night and day" for a period of three years, using every contact—not just official occasions—for instruction and warning.

> In the present context, admonishing involves warning believers about the subtle, ongoing dangers of false teachers and the all-too-common human tendency to become inattentive.

All good teachers reinforce their teaching by constant repetition. As a skilled teacher, Paul persistently and consistently warned the people of the coming battles against the forces of darkness for the truths of the gospel, from his first encounter with them until he had to leave.

Tearful Admonition

Furthermore, his "tears" authenticated the apostle's admonitions. He had seen the terrible damage to local congregations perpetrated by false teachers. A good shepherd loves his sheep, especially the little lambs. His eye is on every single sheep. He knows the weak and the strong, the vulnerable and the stable. It grieves him to see his flock torn to pieces and eaten, or to see the flock scattered over cold, lonely mountains.

Paul loved the Lord Jesus and all his beloved people. So it was with tears that he warned them of "fierce wolves" and the deadly consequences of their attacks: "For many, of whom I have often told you and now tell you even with tears, walk as enemies of the cross of Christ" (Phil. 3:18).

Finally, his admonition was inclusive. He never ceased "to admonish everyone." No one was too insignificant for him to warn and care for. All were under his watching eyes. May we too warn and equip fellow believers with such thoroughness and tearful compassion.

Easily Led Astray

One reason Paul had to caution the believers night and day is that people can be easily fooled by silver-tongued preachers, and their twisted logic, and bombastic promises. In the Old Testament, the scheming, charismatic politician Absalom, King David's son, misled the people of Israel. Through his cunning deceit and flattery, Absalom conspired to sway the nation to turn on their beloved King David, to attempt to kill him, and make Absalom king (2 Sam. 15–18). This is a good example of how easily people can be fooled by a captivating personality who promises a bright, new future.

In the case of the newly planted churches of Galatia, Judaizing teachers visited soon after Paul left. They tried to draw away the disciples from the gospel proclaimed by Paul, and instead to convince them to follow their works-based gospel. In near disbelief, Paul wrote to the "foolish Galatians" (Gal. 3:1):

> I am astonished that *you are so quickly deserting him* who called you in the grace of Christ and are turning to a different gospel—not that there is another one, but *there are some who trouble you and want to distort the gospel of Christ.* (Gal. 1:6–7)

Look at what Paul said about the gullibility of the wayward Corinthians:

> But I am afraid that as the serpent deceived Eve by his cunning, your thoughts *will be led astray* from a sincere and pure devotion to Christ. For if someone comes and proclaims another Jesus than the one we proclaimed, or if you receive a different spirit from the one you received, or if you accept a different gospel from the one you accepted, *you put up with it* readily enough. (2 Cor. 11:3–4)

Paul warned the Christians in Rome:

> I appeal to your, brothers, to *watch out* for those who cause divisions and create obstacles contrary to the doctrine that you have been taught; avoid them. For such persons do not serve our Lord Christ, but their own appetites, and *by smooth talk and flattery they deceive the hearts of the naïve.* (Rom. 16:17–18)

These examples demonstrate just how much we are like sheep, easily getting lost, confused, or led astray (Ps. 119:176). "All we like sheep have gone astray," Isaiah reminds us (Isa. 53:6). Sheep can be easily fooled, and can be lazy.

On a Sunday morning in a well-known church, the pastor preached a sermon introducing new doctrines that varied sharply with the church's foundational theological beliefs. He taught these new doctrines without ever discussing them with the church elders. But what was even more appalling was that no one challenged the preacher or said a word! The congregation just sat there like dumb sheep, being led astray. Instead of scores of people lining up to question the pastor after his sermon, in order to "contend for the faith that was once for all delivered to the saints" (Jude 3), the people raced out, I suppose, to get to their favorite restaurants for lunch before other church crowds got there first.

The problem was that this church had elders who were not biblical elders. They were not men of the Word, protectors of the gospel, guardians of the flock. They were "board" elders—passive and unqualified to protect the flock from erroneous teaching. They did not recognize danger. They were not discerning shepherds, although they did know all the best Sunday restaurants in town.

Take Action

The reason elders must be alert is, not just to be informed, but so they are ready to act. Both imperative commands, "pay careful attention" (v. 28), and "be alert" (v. 32), imply action. A good overseer-watchman-shepherd is never passive but always alert. He knows the necessity of acting quickly and decisively in the face of danger.

> To be given the authority by God to govern and protect, and to not act at the moment of crisis would be a colossal failure of leadership.

Since the Holy Spirit placed the elders as overseers to shepherd the church, *they have the God-given authority to stop, silence, rebuke, and discipline false teachers* (1 Tim. 1:3; Titus 1:7, 11, 13). To be given the authority by God to govern and protect, and to not act at the moment of crisis would be a colossal failure of leadership.

"A Little Leaven": Leaders who will not remove false teachers from the local church or denomination are inviting far worse problems like the loss of the life-giving gospel of Christ and defections by the faithful. Paul reminds us, "A little leaven leavens the whole lump" (1 Cor. 5:6). And again, "Do not be deceived: 'Bad company ruins good morals'" (1 Cor. 15:33). When we compromise with false teaching or refuse to take decisive action to stop it, the error spreads quickly like gangrene and infects the spiritual health of the whole church or denomination. This is an old story, repeated over and over in local churches and major denominations.

Stay Informed: To "be alert" means to work at being aware of current issues and cultural trends that, unless confronted, will eventually seep into the local church and cause conflict and division.

Stay up-to-date on cultural shifts in society and trendy new ideas challenging Christians. Utilize the many audio and printed resources available to help busy people stay informed of important changes in society and in the larger Christian community. These resources will help you to be more conscientious, knowledgeable, discerning, and awake to the many cultural dangers that face people in your local church.

SATAN'S STRATEGY OF LIES

None of Paul's warnings or exhortations to vigilance make sense unless there is a real enemy who seeks to destroy God's household. Paul was not suffering from paranoid delusions nor did he conceive imaginary adversaries. There really are "cosmic powers," "spiritual forces of evil in the heavenly places," "schemes of the devil," and "flaming darts of the evil one" (Eph. 6:11, 12, 16). Paul accurately identified the enemy as Satan, the devil, and all his demonic host. They are as real as the earth upon which we stand and live.[11]

> If there is no real being called Satan, then Jesus Christ was self-deceived and not the perfect incarnate Son of God.

Jesus and Satan

No one understood or faced the reality of Satan or his diabolical strategy better than Jesus Christ our Lord: "The reason the Son of God appeared was to destroy the works of the devil" (1 John 3:8). The devil's works and character were best summarized by Jesus, when he called him "a liar and the father of lies," and "a murderer from the beginning" (John 8:44). Jesus also named Satan "the evil one" who snatches away the Word of God when people hear it preached (Matt. 13:19), "the ruler of this world" (John 12:31; 14:30; 16:11), and "the enemy" of all believers (Matt. 13:39). If there is no real being called Satan, then Jesus Christ was self-deceived and not the perfect incarnate Son of God.

The Bible and Satan

The Bible unapologetically describes Satan as "the deceiver of the whole world" (Rev. 12:9), "who disguises himself as an angel of light" (2 Cor. 11:14). He is the ancient "serpent" who deceived Eve (2 Cor. 11:3) and who holds "the power of death" (Heb. 2:14). He is "the tempter" (1 Thess. 3:5), the "adversary" (1 Peter 5:8), "the great dragon" (Rev. 12:9), "the accuser of our brothers" (Rev. 12:10), and "a roaring lion" (1 Peter 5:8). He is able to set snares to capture people in order "to do his will" (2 Tim. 2:26), and he can hinder the Lord's servants (1 Thess. 2:18).

The Strategy: Satan's core strategy is to fill the world with lies—philosophical lies, economic lies, political lies, and religious lies. He is the cruel mastermind behind all that is false and destructive to the human race. He is everywhere sowing the poisonous seeds of his lies, ever since the day he first lied to Eve. "Wheresoever God buildeth his church," says sixteenth-century reformer Thomas Becon, "there the devil also buildeth his chapel."[12]

Victory in Jesus

Although "the whole world lies in the power of the evil one" (1 John 5:19), it is Jesus Christ who is "King of kings and Lord of lords" (Rev. 19:16). He has already crushed the head of the serpent. Satan's days are numbered, and he is doomed to the lake of fire forever (Rev. 20:10).

John encourages us by reminding us that "he who is in you is greater than he who is in the world" (1 John 4:4). By the enabling power of the Holy Spirit, be alert to Satan's many counterfeit gospels. Don't feed in his pastures of poisonous weeds. Shepherd your flock to higher ground, still, clear waters, and pastures filled with soul-nourishing food provided by God in his Word.

KEY POINTS TO REMEMBER

1. It is your duty to detect and fight off wolves in sheep's clothing.

2. Prepare your people to resist the pressure from secular society to conform to its standards of morality, sexuality, gender identity, marriage, truth, and secularized religion.

3. You have the God-given authority to stop, silence, rebuke, and discipline false teachers. To be given that authority by God and to not act in the moment of crisis would be a colossal failure of leadership.

4. Paul's warnings and exhortations to vigilance make sense because there is a real enemy who seeks to destroy God's people.

5. Use the audio and printed resources available to help you be more knowledgeable, discerning, and awake to the many present cultural dangers facing the families of your church.

---

[1] This quotation is commonly attributed to Benjamin Franklin. Cf. Benjamin Franklin Quotes. BrainyQuote.com, BrainyMedia Inc, 2020, https://www.brainyquote.com/quotes/benjamin_franklin_138217, accessed June 30, 2020.

[2] J. B. Phillips, *The New Testament in Modern English.*

[3] David E. Garland, *1 Corinthians*, BECNT (Grand Rapids: Baker Academic, 2003), 8.

[4] 1 Tim. 1:20; 2 Tim. 2:17.

[5] J. Gresham Machen, *Christianity & Liberalism* (New York: Macmillan, 1923; repr., Grand Rapids: Eerdmans, 1946), 2, 6–7. Liberal Protestantism "differs from Christianity in its view of God, of man, of the seat of authority and of the way of salvation. . . . Christianity is being attacked from within by a movement which is anti-Christian to the core" (173).

[6] BDAG, s.v. "γρηγορέω," 208 (see Matt. 26:41; 1 Cor. 16:13; Col. 4:2; 1 Peter 5:8). The verb appears frequently in the context of the Lord's imminent return for his people. We are thus to be living in such a way that demonstrates we are prepared and ready for his return (Matt. 24:42–43; 25:13; Mark 13:34–35, 37; 14:38; Luke 12:37; 1 Thess. 5:6, 10; Rev. 3:2–3; 16:5).

[7] David Gooding, *True to the Faith, The Acts of the Apostles: Defending and Defining the Gospel* (Coleraine, N. Ireland: Myrtlefield Trust, 2013), 426.

[8] Gooding, *True to the Faith*, 422.

[9] BDAG, s.v. "νουθετέω," 679, "to counsel about avoidance or cessation of an improper course of conduct, admonish, warn, instruct." Also see *NIDNTTE*, "νουθετέω," 3:424–425.

[10] J. Behm, "νουθετέω," *TDNT*, 4 (1967): 1019.

[11] See 1 Chron. 21:1; Job 2:1–4, 6–7; Zech. 3:1–2.

[12] Thomas Becon, *Prayers and Other Pieces of Thomas Becon, Chaplain to Archbishop Cranmer, Prebendary of Canterbury*, ed. John Ayre (Wipf and Stock Publishers 2004), 401

CHAPTER 10

Entrusting the Elders to God and His Word

And now I commend you to God and to the word of his grace,
which is able to build you up and to give you the inheritance
among all those who are sanctified.
(Acts 20:32)

Paul was leaving his coworkers behind in the spiritually dark city of Ephesus. Biblical commentator R. H. Charles accurately remarks that "Ephesus was . . . a hotbed of every kind of cult and superstition."[1] Emperor worship (the imperial cult) thrived in Ephesus and was a required duty of every citizen. Refusing to offer incense to the Roman emperor led to the persecution of many of the first Christians. Furthermore, Ephesus was a port city and a prosperous trade center, known for its immorality. It was not easy to be a disciple of Jesus Christ in the hostile, pagan city of Ephesus.

In his classic allegory, *Pilgrim's Progress*, John Bunyan described the visit of his heroes, Christian and Faithful, to the fair in the town of Vanity. Vanity Fair is a picture of this world with all its sinful human attractions, such as brothels, gambling, drunkenness, greed, murder, and violence. It is for good reason that the New Testament scholar, William Barclay, referred to Ephesus as "the Vanity Fair of the Ancient World."[2]

Although Paul was leaving, he knew that God and his Word would be there to sustain the elders. With full confidence, Paul could entrust the elders to no better source of strength and safekeeping than to the eternal, faithful God and the life-giving, soul-nourishing "word of his grace."

ENTRUSTED TO GOD

As their missionary founder, Paul can say: "And now I commend you to God and to the word of his grace." The Greek verb used for "commend" means "to entrust for safekeeping, give over, entrust."[3] More specifically, in this context, it is to "entrust someone to the care or protection of someone."[4]

"I am God, and there is no other; I am God, and there
is none like me." Isaiah 46:9

The God of the Bible

The God to whom Paul commits the elders is not some undefined, shadowy figure hiding in the sky. He is not one god among the many gods in the Roman pantheon of gods. Nor is he Aristotle's "unmoved mover." He is the infinite, personal, triune God of the Bible. He is the sovereign Creator and Sustainer of the entire universe. Without him nothing exists or holds together. He is in absolute control of all life's affairs and details. He is the self-existing, self-revealing almighty God. "Great is the Lord . . . his greatness is unsearchable" (Ps. 145:3). He is the one, true, incomparable God. There is no other god like him. In fact, there is no other god, as God himself declares:

> I am God, and *there is no other*; I am God, and there is none like
> me, declaring the end from the beginning and from ancient
> times things not yet done, saying, "My counsel shall stand, and
> I will accomplish all my purpose." (Isa. 46:9–10)

Moses tells the people of Israel: "For the Lord your God is God of
gods and Lord of lords, the great, the mighty, and the awesome God"
(Deut. 10:17). In the Song of Moses, it is asked: "Who is like you,
majestic in holiness, awesome in glorious deeds, doing wonders?"
(Ex. 15:11).

The Sustaining God of Israel

Paul knew that the God who sustained the Israelites for forty years
in the barren, dry wilderness could sustain these elders as they
shepherded God's flock, even in a city controlled by Satan and his
demonic hosts. Although their beloved apostle and teacher would
not return, they were not left helpless and unprotected. The God of
Abraham, Isaac, and Jacob was with them. They could depend completely on him.

The Old Testament Scriptures emphasize the power of God
to safeguard and provide for his people in the worst possible
circumstances:

> [God] who led you [Israelites] through the great and terrifying
> wilderness, with its fiery serpents and scorpions and thirsty
> ground where there was no water, who brought you water out
> of the flinty rock, who fed you in the wilderness with manna
> that your fathers did not know, that he might humble you and
> test you, to do you good in the end. (Deut. 8:15–16)

Paul firmly believed what the Psalmist proclaimed long ago: "He who
keeps you will not slumber. Behold, he who keeps Israel will neither slumber nor sleep. The Lord is your keeper" (Ps. 121:3–5). Paul
wanted nothing more than for the Ephesian elders to have a strong,

biblical theology of God, to know his attributes, and to love and obey him. *He wanted them to know God and to trust not in themselves, nor even in their church's missionary founder and beloved apostle, but in God.*

> Paul wanted nothing more than for the elders to have a strong, biblical theology of God, to know his attributes, and to love and obey him.

J. I. Packer, author of the well-known book, *Knowing God*, makes this point:

> Knowing about God is crucially important for the living of our lives. . . . Disregard the study of God, and you sentence yourself to stumble and blunder through life blindfolded, as it were, with no sense of direction and no understanding of what surrounds you. This way you can waste your life and lose your soul.[5]

A. W. Tozer, well-known author of many books on the Christian life, wrote, "There is no study more 'relevant' to the Church in our time than the study of the attributes of God"[6] He further states, "A right conception of God is basic not only to systematic theology but to practical Christian living as well."[7]

Donald Grey Barnhouse, once minister at the Tenth Presbyterian Church in Philadelphia, Pennsylvania, and pioneer in Christian radio, tells an interesting story of his encounter with his former professor Dr. Robert Dick Wilson. Dr. Wilson was a world-recognized scholar who dedicated his life to proving the reliability of the Hebrew Bible, even learning forty-five languages, and the languages into which the Hebrew Bible was translated before AD 600.

Dr. Wilson went to hear Donald Barnhouse speak to the student body at his former seminary in order to see what kind of God his former student preached, a big-god or a little-god. Barnhouse recalls:

I learned the idea of a great God and a little God from my old professor of Hebrew, Robert Dick Wilson, who was one of the intellectual glories of Princeton Theological Seminary in the great days of Warfield, Davis, Machen, and the others. After I had been away from the Seminary for about twelve years, I was invited back to preach to the students. Old Dr. Wilson came into Miller Chapel and sat down near the front while I set forth the Word of God. At the close of the meeting the old gentleman came up to me, cocked his head on one side in his characteristic way, extended his hand, and said, "If you come back again, I will not come to hear you preach. I only come once. I am glad that you are a big-godder. When my boys [former seminary students] come back, I come to see if they are big-godders or little-godders, and then I know what their ministry will be." I asked him to explain, and he replied: "Well, some men have a little god, and they are always in trouble with him. He [God] can't do any miracles. He can't take care of the inspiration and transmission of the Scripture to us. He doesn't intervene on behalf of His people. They have a little god and I call them little-godders. Then there are those who have a great God. He speaks and it is done. He commands and it stands fast. He knows how to show Himself strong on behalf of them that fear him. You have a great God; and He will bless your ministry." He paused a moment and smiled, and said, "God bless you," and turned, and walked out.

I am certainly glad that I do have a great God. I have the God who knows all, is all-powerful, unchanging, eternal, never-failing. My God has never made a mistake. He has never been surprised by anything that happened, for He has always known and decreed all things. He knows the end from the beginning.[8]

Paul was a "big-godder." And he committed the elders to a big God, who was more than capable of watching over them as they labored in the dark, hostile city of Ephesus.

Trusting God

One of the major themes of the Old Testament is that God is faithful. He keeps his covenant promises: "The steadfast love of the Lord never ceases; his mercies never come to an end; they are new every morning; *great is your faithfulness*" (Lam. 3:22–23).

Since the God of Scripture is absolutely trustworthy and faithfully keeps his covenant promises, *the fundamental principle that every child of God must learn—and relearn throughout life—is daily, moment-by-moment trust in God.*

Those who fear God know the bedrock principle of godly living: "Trust in the Lord with all your heart, and do not lean on your own understanding. In all your ways acknowledge him, and he will make straight your paths" (Prov. 3:5–6). The Psalmist David repeatedly spoke of the believer's need to trust in the Lord because he is the only sovereign Lord over all of life's details. He lovingly cares for all his people; and he is wise and good. "Some trust in chariots and some in horses, but we trust in the name of the Lord our God" (Ps. 20:7).

Paul's Crisis Experience: While facing a near-death experience in the city of Ephesus, even the veteran missionary Paul had to relearn the principal lesson of trust in God when all human resources failed:

> For we do not want you to be unaware, brothers, of the affliction we experienced in Asia. For we were so utterly burdened beyond our strength that we despaired of life itself. Indeed, we felt that we had received the sentence of death. But that was to make us rely not on ourselves but on God who raises the dead. He delivered us from such a deadly peril, and he will deliver us. On him we have set our hope that he will deliver us again. (2 Cor. 1:8–10)

We all have to learn and relearn the lesson that none of us are "sufficient in ourselves to claim anything as coming from us, but our sufficiency is from God" (2 Cor. 3:5).

The Christian life is a life of faith and trust in the faithful and trustworthy God of the Bible. The troubles, failures, and crises that will eventually come upon you as a shepherd of the Lord's people are to be used to drive you to greater knowledge and trust in God, to prayer, and to a deeper and more intimate relationship with the living God. *God is honored when his children trust him in adversity and suffering.*

Elders, the task that God has assigned to you is not easy; you cannot do this in your own strength. So you must learn to trust in God for the wisdom and strength that only he can graciously provide.

> You will not have a sound theology of God
> or of Christ if you do not read and know
> God's written Word.

The Self-Revealing God of Scripture

But you cannot trust in God if you do not know him. And the only way to know God is through his own self-revelation in the Old and New Testament Scriptures. If you want to know God and trust him more, read the Old Testament as well as the New Testament. The God of the Old Testament is the very same God of the New. The Jesus of the New Testament is the Jesus predicted in the Old Testament. No one makes this point more precisely than Jesus himself:

> Then he said to them, "These are my words that I spoke to you while I was still with you, that *everything written about me in the Law of Moses and the Prophets and the Psalms must be fulfilled."* Then he opened their minds to understand the Scriptures. (Luke 24:44–45)

You will not have a sound theology of God or of Christ if you do not read and know God's written Word. You will not be able to teach people about God or Christ our wonderful Savior, if you are ignorant of his Book.

ENTRUSTED TO GOD'S WORD

Although Paul refers to "God" and "the word of his grace," grammatically, he has one concept in view.[9] God works in and through "the word of his grace," that is, the gospel message, the Word of God. It is the divine power of God working through the Word of God that is "able to build" up the elders in their faith and to give them the eternal inheritance shared among all the saints of God. Paul entrusted them to the absolute best authority, God's Word. You too must find your strength and rest in the eternal God and his life-transforming, life-building Word.

> You too must find your strength
> and rest in the eternal God and
> his life-transforming, life-building Word.

The Word (*Logos*)

Paul entrusted the elders "to the word (λόγος [*logos*]) of his grace." This phrase is one of several used in the New Testament to describe the great and glorious truths of the gospel message. This same phrase appears in Acts 14:3: "So [Paul and Barnabas] remained for a long time [in Iconium], speaking boldly for the Lord, who bore witness to *the word of his grace*." Back in Acts 20:24, Paul referred to the gospel as "the gospel of the grace of God."

The phrase "the word of his grace" emphasizes the free, saving grace of God in providing salvation through his Son for undeserving sinners. No one states this profound truth better than Paul: "For by grace you have been saved through faith. And this is not your own doing; it is the gift of God, not a result of works, so that no one may boast" (Eph. 2:8–9).

Here are similar *logos* statements for the gospel. Each has its own special nuance:

- "The word" (Acts 4:4)
- "Your word" (Acts 4:29)
- "The word of God" (Acts 6:2, 7)
- "The word of the Lord" (Acts 8:25)
- "The message [*logos*] of this salvation" (Acts 13:26)
- "The word of the cross" (1 Cor. 1:18)
- "The message [*logos*] of reconciliation" (2 Cor. 5:19)
- "The word of truth, the gospel of your salvation" (Eph. 1:13)
- "The word of life" (Phil. 2:16)
- "The word of the truth, the gospel" (Col. 1:5)
- "The word of Christ" (Col. 3:16)

The Ephesian elders had heard "the word of his grace" through Paul's preaching. By believing this divine message from God, they received forgiveness of sins, justification before God, adoption into God's family, and the gift of the Holy Spirit of God. Only God's supernatural message of grace has divine power to cause a spiritually dead person to be born anew. In the words of Peter:

> You have been *born again*, not of perishable seed but of imperishable, *through the living and abiding word of God*; . . . the word of the Lord remains forever. And *this word is the good news* that was preached to you. (1 Peter 1:23, 25)

ABLE TO BUILD YOU UP SPIRITUALLY

The Ephesian elders were not only saved through the message of God's saving grace, that same gospel message would also build them up and sustain them. God actively works through the gospel message to protect, sanctify, and build up his people. "After all," writes Jeff Robinson, "the Spirit of God uses the Word of God to conform us to the Son of God (John 17:17)."[10]

"The Spirit of God uses the Word of God to conform us to the Son of God (John 17:17)." —Jeff Robinson

Working through his Word—the gospel message of saving grace—God is able to build[11] you up in your holy faith and strengthen you for the arduous task of teaching Scripture and protecting the church from false teachers. God's written Word has divine power:

- To help you know yourself better
- To mature and grow you into Christlike character
- To increase your love for God
- To motivate and energize you to serve
- To strengthen you in your battle against sin
- To give you a greater knowledge of God and his ways
- To make you a wise and discerning leader
- To help you endure suffering

Take a moment to consider carefully the amazing claim that Scripture makes about itself. What does this passage mean for you personally and in your work as a shepherd elder?

> *All Scripture is breathed out by God and profitable* for teaching, for reproof, for correction, and for training in righteousness, that the man of God may be complete, *equipped for every good work.* (2 Tim. 3:16–17)

All Scripture originated from within the mind and heart of God. What the Scripture says, God says. The "Scripture" is "the word of God" (John 10:35), and God's Word "is truth" (John 17:17). "The Bible," declares Kevin DeYoung, "can no more fail, falter, or err, than God himself can fail, falter, or err."[12] The Scripture has divine, binding authority. There is nothing else like it in all the world. Jesus believed it, taught it, and lived it. It is one of the greatest treasures God has given us.

Ask yourself: Do you trust the Bible? Do you believe it to be the Word of God? Is it truthful? Paul was confident that God-breathed Scripture was perfectly sufficient to provide guidance, knowledge, encouragement, and comfort to the hard-working Ephesian shepherds, and to you as well. Commenting on 2 Timothy 3:16, John Stott asks:

> Do we hope, either in our own lives or in our teaching ministry, to overcome error and grow in truth, to overcome evil and grow in holiness? Then it is to Scripture that we must turn, for Scripture is "profitable" for these things. . . . Indeed, Scripture is the chief means which God employs to bring "the man of God" to maturity.[13]

There is simply nothing else in all the world so able to build you up in your most holy faith and strengthen your shepherding ability than God-breathed-out Scripture.

> "Indeed, Scripture is the chief means which
> God employs to bring 'the man of God'
> to maturity." —John Stott

The Battle for the Bible

God-breathed Scripture is the bedrock of everything we believe, say, and do. The sixteenth-century reformers built their theology firmly on *Sola Scriptura*, Scripture alone. Associate editor of *Expositor Magazine* Dustin Benge puts the issue this way:

> Everything hinges on your view of Scripture. Either Scripture will be the lens through which you view the world, or the world (science, politics, worldview, etc.) will be the lens through which you view Scripture. Ultimately one or the other will be your authority.[14]

171

Satan, the implacable archenemy of Jesus Christ, knows that he must do everything within his power to destroy the foundation of the Christian faith, the Bible. As Jonathan Edwards so memorably wrote:

> The devil has ever shown a mortal spite and hatred towards that holy book the Bible; he has done all in his power to extinguish that light . . . He is enraged against the Bible, and hates every word in it.[15]

Theologian John W. Robbins best articulates the devil's aim this way:

> But the history of the Church also demonstrates that there is one perennial and recurring battle: the battle for the Bible. The Devil, with diabolical wisdom, continually returns to attack the first principle, the starting point, the axiom of Christianity: the Bible. He knows that if he can destroy, distort, or smother that Word, then he need not confuse men's minds about the Trinity or the incarnation. By destroying the foundation for those doctrines, he destroys them too.[16]

Are you aware of this "one perennial and recurring battle" for the Bible? You will most certainly face this battle someday. Stand firm! Only the Word of God can "build you up" and equip you to be a skilled, Christlike leader and teacher of God's people.

ABLE TO GIVE YOU THE INHERITANCE

We all like to dream about receiving a large, surprise inheritance from a long-lost relative. Once I did receive an inheritance from an aunt whom I had not seen in forty years. But by the time the lawyers, the bank, and the state tax assessors all got their share, there wasn't much left for me.

This is not the case for the believer. Paul says, "in [Christ] we have obtained an inheritance" (Eph. 1:11), and there is no tax or lawyer fee on this inheritance. As Peter says so eloquently, it is "an inheritance that is imperishable, undefiled, and unfading, kept in heaven for you" (1 Peter 1:4).

The message of God's grace "is able . . . to give" us an "inheritance among all those who are sanctified."[17] What supernatural, divine power there is in the message of his saving grace, that it can promise people an eternal, heavenly inheritance. This is not an earthly, temporal inheritance that fades away in time. This inheritance is the full salvation promised by God. All believers in Christ are among "those who are to inherit salvation" (Heb. 1:14). All who believe in Jesus Messiah "will inherit eternal life" (Matt. 19:29; also Titus 3:7).

> What a powerful message this is, that God has given his people an eternal, heavenly inheritance.

Eternal life will not be lived on an airy cloud in the sky. It will be lived in God's magnificent kingdom on the newly created earth, in "the holy city Jerusalem coming down out of heaven from God, having the glory of God, its radiance like a most rare jewel, like a jasper, clear as crystal" (Rev. 21:10–11). We will live on the new earth with our new imperishable bodies, like our Lord's imperishable, resurrected body. What a message! What a promise! There's nothing else like it in all the world's religions or philosophies. Now believe it!

A Guaranteed Inheritance

Paul assures us that the indwelling Holy Spirit is "the guarantee of our inheritance until we acquire possession of it, to the praise of his glory" (Eph. 1:14). Yes, we should cry out loudly, "to the praise of his glory"! As children adopted into the family of God, we are now "heirs of God and fellow heirs with Christ" of all that is his for eternity (Rom. 8:17). This is the final blessing of our salvation.

A Shared Inheritance

This inheritance is not something we possess selfishly or enjoy alone in isolation from others. This inheritance is shared "among all those who are sanctified" by the blood of God's own Son. In Scripture, "those who are sanctified" are called "saints," that is, "holy ones," "separate ones," "consecrated ones." Only by God's saving grace can rebellious, ungodly creatures be made holy before a holy God. Thus Paul urged his readers to be "giving thanks to the Father, who has qualified you to share in the inheritance of the saints in light" (Col. 1:12).

Upon Paul's conversion on the Damascus Road, Jesus commissioned him to reach the Gentile world with the message of the gospel, which included the amazing promise of "a place among those who are sanctified":

> I am sending you to open their eyes, so that they [the Gentiles] may turn from darkness to light and from the power of Satan to God, that they may receive forgiveness of sins and *a place among those who are sanctified by faith in me.* (Acts 26:17–18)

The only way to be assured that you have "a place among those who are sanctified" is by "faith" in the crucified, risen, exalted Lord Jesus Christ. Those who are sanctified include the full community of God's redeemed people, past, present, and future, "from every tribe and language and people and nation" (Rev. 5:9). Our secure, eternal future together is best described at the conclusion of the Bible:

> And I [John] heard a loud voice from the throne saying, "Behold, the dwelling place of God is with man. He will dwell with them, and they will be his people, and God himself will be with them as their God. He will wipe away every tear from their eyes, and death shall be no more, neither shall there be mourning, nor crying, nor pain anymore, for the former things have passed away." And he who was seated on the throne said, "Behold I am making all things new." (Rev. 21:3–5)

What more exhilarating, breathtaking promise than that God himself will dwell eternally with all those who are sanctified by the blood of Jesus?

Anything we lose or are deprived of here on earth in terms of material possessions, or whatever we suffer for serving Christ's people is incomparable to the eternal treasures and glories of the new heaven and earth.

The Divine Perspective

This eternal inheritance puts all our labor of shepherding God's people into eternal perspective. Anything we lose or are deprived of here on earth in terms of material possessions, or whatever we suffer for serving Christ's people is incomparable to the eternal treasures and glories of the new heaven and earth.

On one occasion, Peter asked Jesus what he and the other disciples would gain from their sacrifice of leaving everything to follow Jesus. Jesus answered:

> Truly, I say to you, there is no one who has left house or brothers or sisters or mother or father or children or lands, for my sake and for the gospel, who will not *receive a hundredfold now in this time*, houses and brothers and sisters and mothers and children and lands, with persecutions, *and in the age to come eternal life*. (Mark 10:29–30)

Peter's question reminds me of the oft-repeated quotation by Jim Elliot, a gifted and godly young missionary. In attempting to give the gospel to the primitive tribe of Auca Indians living in the dense jungles of Ecuador, he and four other missionaries were killed by Auca warriors. But while in college, Jim Elliot had kept a journal documenting his spiritual development. His journal contained numerous statements that have now become well-known to the Christian community. One of his most memorable quotes is: "He is no fool who gives what he cannot keep to gain what he cannot lose."[18]

We are all pilgrims here upon earth. This present earth is not our final home. Someday it will all be burned up by God's just judgment. But for now, we are journeying to our permanent dwelling, the new earth and the unshakable, eternal kingdom of God and of Christ.

> "He is no fool who gives what he cannot keep to gain what he cannot lose." —Jim Elliot

Keep this awe-inspiring truth front and center in your mind when you get discouraged or wonder, "What is the purpose of all my hard work and sacrifice?" What you need to remember is that what you are seeing now is only temporal, but what is unseen is eternal and beyond our human imagination:

> For this light momentary affliction is preparing for us an eternal weight of glory beyond all comparison, as we look not at things that are seen but to the things that are unseen. For the things that are seen are transient, but the things that are unseen are eternal. (2 Cor. 4:17–18)

Even though Paul would no longer be with the elders, they would know and be assured that he had entrusted them to the best possible source of strength and safekeeping—the eternal, faithful God and the life-giving, soul-nourishing "word of his grace." Upon this knowledge they must act.

KEY POINTS TO REMEMBER

1. The fundamental principle that we must all learn and re-learn throughout life is this: daily, moment-by-moment trust in the living God and his written promises.

2. You need to have a strong, biblical theology of the person of God or you will not be able to trust him when the trials come.

3. You cannot trust in God if you do not know him, and the only way to know him is through the regular reading and study of the Bible.

4. Scripture has the power to build you up in your most holy faith and make you a more biblically-minded, skilled pastor-elder.

5. You need to keep the awe-inspiring truth about your eternal inheritance in mind when you get discouraged or wonder, "What is the purpose of all my hard work and sacrifice?"

---

[1] R. H. Charles, *The Revelation of St. John*, ICC (New York: Scribner, 1920), 1:48.

[2] William Barclay, *Letters to the Seven Churches* (Nashville: Abingdon, 1957), 11; cf. John Bunyan, *The Pilgrim's Progress: From This World to That Which Is to Come* (Westwood, NJ: Barbour, n.d.), 97–102.

[3] BDAG, s.v. "παρατίθημι," 772. See also Luke 23:46; 1 Peter 4:19. To entrust the gospel to someone for safekeeping and transmission, see 1 Tim. 1:18; 2 Tim. 2:2. The NRSV, NASB, NKJV also render the verb as "commend;" the NIV and CSB translate the verb as "commit," and the NET, NLT have "entrust."

[4] Ibid, 772. Some ten years before Paul's Miletus discourse, as Paul and Barnabas were departing from their newly planted churches in Galatia (AD 47), they "committed" their newly appointed elders into the Lord's care by means of prayer and fasting: "And when they had appointed elders for them in every church, with prayer and fasting [Paul and Barnabas] *committed them* to the Lord in whom they had believed" (Acts 14:23). Prayerfully committing the churches and their leaders into God's care upon their departure would teach their new converts to trust in God and rely fully on "the living and abiding word of God" (1 Peter 1:23).

[5] J. I. Packer, *Knowing God* (Downers Grove, IL: InterVarsity, 1973; repr. 1993), 19.

[6] A. W. Tozer, *The Knowledge of the Holy* (New York: Harper & Row, 1961), 6.

[7] Tozer, *The Knowledge of the Holy*, 10.

[8] Donald Grey Barnhouse, *Romans, vol. 3: God's Remedy (Rom. 3:21-4:25)* [1954; repr. Grand Rapids: Eerdmans, 1983], 340–341.

[9] God and the word of his grace is a hendiadys, that is, the expression of a single idea with two words connected by "and." See C. K. Barrett, *The Acts of the Apostles*, ICC (Edinburgh, T&T Clark, 1998), 2:980–981; Eckhard J. Schnabel, *Acts*, ECNT (Grand Rapids, Zondervan, 2012), 850.

[10] Jeff Robinson, https://www.thegospelcoalition.org/article/5-reasons-to-read-the-entire-bible-in-2016/. Accessed September 18, 2020.

[11] BDAG, s.v. "οἰκοδομέω," 696, "to help improve ability to function in living responsibly and effectively, strengthen, build up, make more able."

[12] Kevin DeYoung, *Taking God at His Word* (Wheaton, IL: Crossway, 2014), 119.

[13] John R. W. Stott, *Guard the Gospel: The Message of 2 Timothy* (Downers Grove, IL: InterVarsity, 1973), 103.

[14] https://twitter.com/DustinBenge/status/1275461899916849159. Accessed June 23, 2020. Dustin W. Benge is also provost and professor at Union School of Theology, Bridgend, Wales.

[15] Jonathan Edwards, "The Distinguishing Marks of a Work of the Spirit of God," in *The Great Awakening*, ed., C. C. Goen, *The Works of Jonathan Edwards*, vol. 4 (New Haven: Yale, 1972), 254.

[16] John W. Robbins, "Foreword," to Gordon Clark, *God's Hammer: The Bible and Its Critics* (Jefferson, MD: Trinity Foundation, 1982).

[17] An eternal inheritance: κληρονομία (*klēronomia*), Eph. 1:14; 5:5; Col. 3:24; Heb. 9:15; 1 Peter 1:4. Also Col. 1:12 (κλῆρος [*klēros*]).

[18] Elisabeth Elliot, *Shadow of the Almighty: The Life and Testament of Jim Elliot* (New York: HarperCollins, 1958), 15, 108.

CHAPTER 11

Maintaining
Financial Integrity

I coveted no one's silver or gold or apparel.
You yourselves know that these hands ministered
to my necessities and to those who were with me.
(Acts 20:33–34)

After Paul entrusted the elders "to God and to the word of his grace," you might think that Paul had reached the end of his discourse, but not so. Instead, he goes on to make *a concluding statement about his own attitude and general policy regarding money and the care of needy members within the believing community.* He expected the elders to take special note of these concerns. He wanted them to know that care for the weak was a part of the shepherding, oversight task.

Nothing is more apt to bring sinister charges against the servants of the Lord than how they handle other people's money. Knowing this, Paul's farewell included a disavowal of greedy motives or exploitation of the flock: "I coveted no one's silver or gold or apparel" (v. 33). Few people can honestly make such a bold, open-hearted confession.

As you read this chapter, keep in mind the worldwide explosion of the health-and-wealth gospel, which in no way resembles Paul's gospel. Prosperity preachers daily exploit millions of poverty-stricken, desperate people with their fake healings and get-rich-quick promises. Without shame, these so-called servants of the Lord spend other people's money lavishly, fly on private jets, stay at expensive hotels, spend thousands of dollars on rich foods and drinks, wear luxurious gold and silver jewelry, buy the most expensive clothing, and own lavish mansions and luxury cars.[1] All of this is done in the name of Jesus Christ and the gospel.

Observe now in verses 33–35 the total contrast between the prosperity preachers and Paul the apostle: "I coveted no one's silver or gold or apparel." Paul imitated the Jesus way of life: selfless service to others. It is taking up the cross, not a new Mercedes-Benz.

DISAVOWING ALL GREED

Let me clarify something here. Paul did not say he never *took* anyone's silver or gold, because he did accept support money from the church in Philippi. His claim was even more profound. He was saying that he had no desire[2] for material profit from his converts, even in the form of clothing. Clothing was a valuable possession in the ancient world and was commonly used to distinguish the rich from the poor.

Paul did not see people as dollar signs.

Money did not motivate Paul to serve others. He did not see people as dollar signs. His work at Ephesus was not done for personal financial gain; on the contrary, it nearly cost him everything, including his life.[3] Again, he points the elders to his personal example as a role model for them to follow.

Warnings about the Sin of Greed

Jesus sternly warned his disciples to "be on guard against" the base sin of greed: "Take care and *be on your guard against all covetousness*, for one's life does not consist in the abundance of his possessions" (Luke 12:15). "Be on guard against" the sin of greed because greed deceives the mind and hardens the heart; it is one of the most powerful inner drives known to mankind.

> "One's life does not consist in the
> abundance of his possessions." Luke 12:15

Paul called greed "idolatry" (Eph. 5:5;[4] Col. 3:5[5]). Jesus said, "You cannot serve God and money" (Luke 16:13). You cannot be a lover of money and a lover of God.

Greed is at the root of many other terrible sins such as lying, stealing, embezzlement, jealousy, and even murder.[6] Several of my friends—some of whom were widows—have been swindled out of their life savings by so-called Christian brothers selling investment plans that turned out to be Ponzi schemes. Paul understood the many evils of greed, and how greed can destroy a person's moral character. Using the strongest of terms, Paul warns:

> For we brought nothing into the world, and we cannot take anything out of the world. But if we have food and clothing, with these we will be content. But those who desire to be rich *fall into temptation*, into a snare, into many senseless and harmful desires that plunge people into ruin and destruction. For *the love of money is a root of all kinds of evils*. It is through this craving that some have *wandered away from the faith* and pierced themselves with many pangs. (1 Tim. 6:7–10)

Money-obsessed pastors have turned many people away from the gospel and from local churches. My own father is an example of one put off by such greed. He did not become a believer in Christ until he was eighty-five years old. Up until his conversion, he viewed all ministers as money grabbers, people who fleeced the flock instead of feeding the flock.

As a young person, my father attended church regularly but the only thing he could recall was the endless, emotional appeals for money. One particular incident caused him to avoid church for the next sixty-five years of his life. He saw the minister take an offering for a new church building project at the funeral of a neighbor! He was so disgusted by this that he stopped attending church entirely. He would joke with me and say, "Doesn't the Bible say, 'Where two or three are gathered together there shall be a collection?'" To him, church was for the gullible.

Paul's Example

How different was Paul! He was not driven by an intense desire for wealth and security. Instead, he described his attitude toward his converts this way: "I seek not what is yours but you . . . I will most gladly spend and be spent for your souls" (2 Cor. 12:14–15). "As poor, yet making many rich; as having nothing, yet possessing everything" (2 Cor. 6:10). He was imitating Jesus who, "though he was rich, yet for your sake he became poor, so that you by his poverty might become rich" (2 Cor. 8:9).

Samuel's Example: Paul's disavowal of greed or exploitation of his converts is similar to that of the godly Old Testament priest and judge, Samuel. At his farewell address to the nation of Israel, Samuel could publicly state that he had never used his official position, title, or influence to take material assets from the faithful:

> "I have walked before you from my youth until this day. Here I am; testify against me before the Lord and before his anointed. Whose ox have I taken? Or whose donkey have I taken? Or whom have I defrauded? Whom have I oppressed? Or from

whose hand have I taken a bribe to blind my eyes with it? Testify against me and I will restore it to you." They [all the men of Israel] said, *"You have not defrauded us or oppressed us or taken anything from any man's hand."* (1 Sam. 12:2b–4)

Like Samuel, Paul called upon the Ephesian elders as witnesses to the fact that he "coveted no one's silver or gold or apparel." When he said "no one's," Paul sincerely meant *no one*—believer or unbeliever, rich or poor, Jew or Greek, man or woman. *Paul took the matter of financial integrity seriously.*

There are four major temptations that Christian leaders face: pride, power, sex, and money.

Paul's Defense: We can detect here, and in other parts of the discourse, an apologetic note. Most likely, after he left Ephesus for Macedonia and Corinth (Acts 20:1–3), Paul's "adversaries" made slanderous accusations against his message, methods, and sincerity. This same pattern of false accusations happened in almost every church and city he left. Paul's opponents would quickly seize upon his departure and start to criticize his gospel and countercultural way of living. As a result, we see in his letters—and here in his address to the elders—a defense of his message and methods. The upside to this is that we learn from Paul's response to these attacks a great deal more about Paul personally and the true content of his message, "the word of truth, the gospel of your salvation" (Eph. 1:13).

Make it your aim to have the same sensitivity to money matters as did Samuel, Paul, and Jesus.

A Powerful Temptation

There are four major temptations that Christian leaders face: pride, power, sex, and money. For some people, money can be a more alluring temptation than sex or power. Stealing church money and misappropriating church funds are widespread problems. Even among the twelve apostles there was a thief. Judas acted as if he cared about the poor, but that was not his true motive. The apostle John explained:

> [Judas] said this, not because he cared about the poor, but because *he was a thief,* and having charge of the moneybag he used to help himself to what was put into it. (John 12:6)

The Old Testament prophet Jeremiah bemoaned the fact that:

> From the least to the greatest of them, *everyone is greedy for unjust gain*; and from prophet to priest, everyone deals falsely. (Jer. 6:13; see also Ezek. 22:27)

Twice Jesus had to cleanse the temple in Jerusalem. The nation's religious leaders had turned God's temple into a merchandise mart, where they could enrich themselves with the people's money. But with holy zeal for God's house, Jesus said, "Is it not written, 'My house shall be called a house of prayer for all nations'? But you have made it a den of robbers" (Mark 11:17).

Things are not much different today. We often hear of high-profile, religious officials caught embezzling church money. In certain parts of the world, the financial exploitation of the people by church leaders is pervasive, a horrible disgrace to our Lord and the true gospel.[7]

God does not want his servants
to be greedy-minded pilferers.

Misappropriation of Money: In most cases, church officials do not steal actual cash. Instead, they misdirect church funds to their own so-called "ministry expenses": meals, travel, vacations, sports activities, and car and home repairs. Unless agreed upon by the congregation and its leaders, all such misappropriation of church funds is "shameful gain" (1 Peter 5:2).

A Biblical Qualification

Knowing the common temptation that church leaders face with managing church funds, Paul established the specific qualification that anyone who aspires to be an elder must "not [be] a lover of money" (1 Tim. 3:3; see also Titus 1:7). The apostle Peter made the same requirement of the Asian elders: they were to "[exercise] oversight . . . [but] not for shameful gain" (1 Peter 5:2).

God does not want his servants to be greedy-minded pilferers. God's standard is this: the leaders of his churches must be concerned with giving rather than getting (v. 35). What a stark contrast to the false teachers who love money and exploit people, "imagining that godliness [or religion] is a means of gain" (1 Tim. 6:5).

> If the church's eldership practices financial transparency, genuine accountability, and sound money management principles, it will bring honor to our Lord and gain the respect of the people.

Financial Integrity: As God's stewards of God's household (Titus 1:7), you have the responsibility to manage church funds in a Christ-honoring way. If the church's eldership practices financial transparency, *genuine* accountability, and sound money management principles, it will bring honor to our Lord and gain the respect of the people. Follow the apostle's example: "For we aim at what is honorable [financially] not only in the Lord's sight *but also in the sight of man*" (2 Cor. 8:21).

WORKING WITH HIS OWN HANDS TO PROVIDE FOR HIS OWN NEEDS

The greediest persons in the world could insist that they "coveted no one's silver or gold," but that would be a lie. Greedy people are self-deceived. But Paul appeals to an unusual aspect of his work in Ephesus to prove his claim: "You yourselves know that these hands ministered to my necessities and to those who were with me" (v. 34). For the third time, Paul directly cites his life example. He wants the elders to remember how he provided for his own livelihood through manual labor and how he was able to give to others.

Even more remarkable is that Paul also supported his coworkers in gospel ministry. Through this assistance, they could work with Paul or travel on his behalf to help struggling churches and to preach the gospel in unreached places. I have seen some of our own church missionaries do the same. They finance indigenous evangelists at their own personal expense, so that these brothers can evangelize and expand the missionary's own outreach and effectiveness. *Effective leaders know how to multiply themselves; they utilize their resources to expand their work through developing coworkers in the gospel.*

Manual Labor

Working with "these hands" was not a token gesture on Paul's part. He labored "night and day." He was tentmaking or doing leather work (Acts 18:3). The phrase "night and day" doesn't mean he literally worked all night and all day; rather, it is a common figure of speech, emphasizing that Paul worked diligently, using both the day time and night time profitably. Diligent workers don't work just eight hours a day and do nothing more in the evening but watch TV.

Paul was not so proud or self-important that he couldn't do manual labor or work with his own hands.

186

Paul also did this while he was in Thessalonica and Corinth. As he says, "We worked night and day, that we might not be a burden to any of you, while we proclaimed to you the gospel of God" (1 Thess. 2:9; also 2 Thess. 3:8–9). "And we labor, working with our own hands" (1 Cor. 4:12; also 1 Cor. 9:6; 2 Cor. 11:7–9; 12:13–18). Paul was not so proud or self-important that he couldn't do manual labor or work with his hands. *In all his labor, he was "serving the Lord with all humility"* (v. 19).

One of our premier Bible commentators, Gordon Fee, points out that, "working with his own hands might well have lowered his [Paul's] status among some of them," that is, among some of the new Thessalonian believers.[8] According to the cultural perspectives of the Thessalonian and Corinthian believers, it was inappropriate for their esteemed teacher to work with his hands to support himself.

However, one of Paul's reasons for self-support was to teach new Christians that their new faith was in many ways countercultural to the norms of Greco-Roman society. In God's eyes, there is no shame in working with one's hands to provide an income while at the same time preaching the gospel free of charge with one's tongue. Paul was not a lesser apostle for engaging in manual labor to support himself in the Lord's work.

"In offering the 'free' gospel 'free of charge' his own ministry becomes a living paradigm of the gospel itself." —Gordon Fee

Foregoing Financial Support

Why did Paul adopt the policy of working to earn his own living? Why not accept financial compensation from his new converts? It seems that Paul did not follow the standard practice of the day. Other apostles and itinerate evangelists received financial support from the churches.[9] There are a number of reasons why Paul chose the general policy of self-support:

1. To prove that he did not covet the people's money or possessions (Acts 20:33–34).

2. To teach the virtue of hard work and self-support. Paul purposely made himself an example of hard work, industry, and self-support so that the new believers would have a role model to imitate (Acts 20:35; 1 Thess. 4:11–12; 2 Thess. 3:7–9).

3. To teach the responsibility to share one's earnings with those in need (Acts 20:35).

4. To remove any "obstacle" to effective evangelism and church planting. "We endure anything rather than put an obstacle in the way of the gospel of Christ" (1 Cor. 9:12b). Paul wanted to remove any suspicion or doubt about his motives as a preacher of the free grace of God to sinners.

5. To not become a financial burden to the new believers, many of whom were not wealthy (1 Thess. 2:9; 2 Thess. 3:8; 2 Cor. 11:9; 12:13–14, 16).

6. To disassociate himself from the itinerate false teachers, who tried to compare themselves to Paul. By providing for his own livelihood, Paul could undercut their criticisms and false claims of being super-apostles (2 Cor. 11:12).

7. To avoid the dangers of patron-client relationships. Refraining from his "right" to material support freed Paul from any kind of human patronage, obligation, false expectation, or restriction. For instance, Paul was not the client or beneficiary of the Corinthians (1 Cor. 9:15–23; 2 Cor. 11:7).

8. To demonstrate his extraordinary relationship to the gospel. Paul's boast or glory was that he freely and voluntarily chose to "present the gospel free of charge" (1 Cor. 9:18; 2 Cor. 11:7). Paul made

himself a living example that the gospel of the grace of God is free to all who will believe. Gordon Fee puts it this way: "In offering the 'free' gospel 'free of charge' his own ministry becomes a living paradigm of the gospel itself."[10]

DEFENDING THE RIGHT TO FINANCIAL SUPPORT

Although Paul's general policy was to earn his own living by manual labor, we do know that he accepted financial gifts from the church at Philippi, and possibly others.[11] While ministering in Thessalonica, the Philippian believers sent financial gifts to Paul to help meet his needs:

> And you Philippians yourselves know that in the beginning of the gospel, when I left Macedonia, no church entered into partnership with me *in giving and receiving*, except you only. Even in Thessalonica *you sent me help for my needs once and again.* (Phil. 4:15–16)

Paul had a unique relationship with the Philippians, demonstrated in their faithful, financial partnership with him in the gospel.

Paul was not a rigid, narrow-minded man. He was flexible and adaptable without violating fundamental principles. Paul was willing to take money from one church (Philippi) but not another (Corinth), because of different circumstances, and his choices were always made based on how they affected the advancement of the gospel.[12]

The Ox and the Laborer

Although Paul did not personally take support from some of his churches, he argued at length in 1 Corinthians 9 for the right[13] of apostles and evangelists to accept financial compensation from those to whom they minister:

> If we have sown spiritual things among you, is it too much if
> we reap material things from you? If others share this *rightful
> claim* on you, do not we even more? (1 Cor. 9:11–12a; also see
> Rom. 15:26–27)

Of special interest to our study are two of the arguments Paul
uses in 1 Corinthians 9 to support this "rightful claim" to financial
compensation for preachers of the gospel:

> Do I say these things on human authority? Does not the Law
> say the same? For it is written in the Law of Moses, *"You shall
> not muzzle an ox when it treads out the grain."* (1 Cor. 9:8–9)

> In the same way, the Lord [Jesus] commanded that those who
> proclaim the gospel *should get their living by the gospel.* (1 Cor.
> 9:14; see Luke 10:7, "for the laborer deserves his wages")

Financial Compensation for Elders Laboring in the Word

Just as Paul defends his "rightful claim" (1 Cor. 9:12) as an apostle
and itinerate evangelist to receive financial compensation, he also
uses the same two scriptural texts (Deut. 25:4 and Luke 10:7) in 1
Timothy 5:18 to defend the rightful claim of certain elders to receive
financial support from their local church:

> Let the elders who rule well be considered worthy of double
> honor, especially *those who labor in preaching and teaching.*
> For the Scripture says, "You shall not muzzle an ox when it
> treads out the grain," and, "The *laborer deserves his wages."* (1
> Tim. 5:17–18)

Paul applied his arguments and instruction regarding the support
of itinerate apostles and evangelists in 1 Corinthians 9 *to the local*

church elders who lead well and, above all, to those who labor in the Word.

The elders who are compensated by the church for their efforts are also to work hard and share their earnings with those in need (vv. 34–35). Indeed, they are to work every bit as hard as the other "tentmaking" elders who have outside employment, families to care for, and heavy church responsibilities.

Acts 20 versus 1 Timothy 5: It appears that Paul assumes that the Ephesian elders would, like himself, work to provide for their own livelihood, and, as a result, share some of their material earnings with their needy brothers and sisters (v. 35).

How, then, are we to interpret 1 Timothy 5:17–18, a passage in which Paul speaks of material compensation for some of the elders in Ephesus? It might seem that there is a conflict between the two passages, but there is not.

In Acts 20, Paul directly addressed the elders face to face, not the congregation at large. He expected them to follow his example of working hard, earning a living, and sharing their resources with those in need. But in 1 Timothy 5:17–18 he directly addressed Timothy and the congregation about honoring their elders. He speaks to an issue not addressed in Acts 20: the congregation's responsibility to honor and, in a few cases, financially support its hard-working elders, especially those who labor at preaching and teaching God's Word.

The two passages should not be pitted against one another, as if some kind of contradiction exists between them. Rather, the instructions complement each other. All elders are to work hard, support themselves, and give to the needy among them. The elder receiving financial compensation from the church is also working hard, supporting himself through gospel labor, and helping others. All are brothers and fellow elders.

WORKING A JOB AND SHEPHERDING
A CONGREGATION

Some people say, "You can't expect a man to work all day, raise a family, and shepherd a local church, too." But that is simply not true. Many people raise families, work, and give substantial hours to community service, athletic activities, home building projects, or religious institutions.

It is positively amazing how much people can accomplish when they are motivated by something they love. I have seen people remodel entire houses in their spare time, or spend mega-hours on hobbies, like rebuilding cars, playing sports, or serving voluntarily on a local city council. I have also seen men discipline themselves to gain a phenomenal knowledge of the Scriptures.

Spiritual Laziness

The real problem lies not in men's limited time, but in false ideas about work, Christian living, and life's priorities. One reason there are so few shepherd elders, or good church elderships, is that, generally speaking, men are spiritually lazy. Spiritual laziness, as well as a lack of self-discipline, is a major reason why most churches never establish a biblical eldership. Too many men are more than willing to let someone else fulfill their spiritual responsibilities, whether it be their wives or the "trained" professionals. Speaking about the absence of men in churches, one author laments that "women go to church; men go to football games."[14] Sadly, there is a lot of truth to that statement.

Spiritual Dedication

A biblical eldership cannot exist in an atmosphere of nominal Christianity. Without biblical Christianity, there can be no biblical eldership. If a New Testament eldership is to function effectively, it must be comprised of men who are firmly committed to our Lord's principles of discipleship. Christian eldership depends on men who seek first the kingdom of God (Matt. 6:33), and who have presented themselves as living sacrifices to God and slaves of the Lord Jesus Christ. From his book *Liberating the Laity*, R. Paul Stevens gives sound biblical advice to tentmaking elders:

> For tentmakers to survive three full-time jobs (work, family and ministry), they must also adopt a sacrificial lifestyle. Tentmakers must live a pruned life and literally find leisure and rest in the rhythm of serving Christ (Matt. 11:28). They must be willing to forego a measure of career achievement and private leisure for the privilege of gaining the prize (Phil. 3:14). Many would like to be tentmakers if they could be wealthy and live a leisurely and cultured lifestyle. But the truth is that a significant ministry in the church and the community can only come by sacrifice.[15]

Although personal sacrifice is required of each individual elder, remember that you do not do the Lord's work alone (see Chapter 7). You and your fellow elders are to shepherd God's flock as a team. In addition, you have the deacons to assist you in your work. You are "to equip the saints for the work of ministry, for building up the body of Christ" (Eph. 4:12). This is the biblical principle of every-member ministry of the body of Christ.

If a New Testament eldership is to function effectively, it must be comprised of men who are firmly committed to our Lord's principles of discipleship.

Giving to the Needy

Paul's disavowal of greed and his example of working with his hands, to provide for his own needs and those of others ministering with him, leads us now to his concluding point which we will examine in the next chapter:

In all things I have shown you that by working hard in this way we must help the weak and remember the words of the Lord Jesus, how he himself said, "It is more blessed to give than to receive." (Acts 20:35)

KEY POINTS TO REMEMBER

1. Take the matter of financial integrity seriously. God does!

2. If you practice financial transparency, genuine account-ability, and sound money management principles as an individual and as an eldership, you will bring honor to our Lord and gain the respect of the people.

3. "For tentmakers to survive three full-time jobs (work, family and ministry), they must also adopt a sacrificial life-style. Tentmakers must live a pruned life and literally find leisure and rest in the rhythm of serving Christ (Matt. 11:28)." — R. Paul Stevens

4. An elder receiving financial compensation from the church is also working hard, supporting himself through gospel labor, and helping others.

5. The entire church body is to be a ministering body to one another. This has often been rightly called "every-member ministry in the body of Christ." The elders are not to do all the work. They are "to equip the saints for the work of ministry, for building up the body of Christ" (Eph. 4:12).

[1] See Costi W. Hinn, *God, Greed, and the (Prosperity) Gospel: How Truth Overwhelms a Life Built on Lies* (Grand Rapids: Zondervan, 2019).

[2] BDAG, s.v. "ἐπιθυμέω," 371, "to have a strong desire to do or secure something, *desire, long for*;" "to desire (strongly), want, lust for" (*NIDNTTE*, s.v. "ἐπιθυμέω," 2:241).

[3] 2 Cor. 1:8–9.

[4] BDAG, s.v. "πλεονέκτης," 824, "one who desires to have more than is due, a greedy person;" "one who is greedy, a covetous person" (*NIDNTTE*, s.v. "πλεονέκτης," 3:780–81).

[5] BDAG, s.v. "πλεονεξία," 824, "the state of desiring to have more than one's due, *greediness, insatiableness, avarice, covetousness*"; "greediness, avarice, covetousness" (*NIDNTTE*, s.v. "πλεονεξία," 3:780–81); "consuming ambition, greed" (*TLNT*, s.v. "πλεονεξία," 3:117).

[6] It is the sin of Achan (Josh. 7:19–21).

[7] See Sunday Bobai Agang, "Radical Islam Is Not the Nigerian Church's Greatest Threat," *Christianity Today* (May 2017), 55–57; *The Cape Town Commitment: A Confession of Faith and a Call to Action* (Bodmin, United Kingdom: The Lausanne Movement, 2011), 55–57, 60.

[8] Gordon D. Fee, *The First and Second Letters to the Thessalonians*, NICNT (Grand Rapids: Eerdmans, 2009), 328.

[9] 1 Cor. 9:4–5.

[10] Gordon D. Fee, *The First Epistle to the Corinthians*, rev. ed., NICNT (Grand Rapids: Eerdmans, 2014), 465.

[11] 2 Cor. 11:8–9.

[12] 2 Cor. 11:7–9; 12:13–14.

[13] BDAG, s.v. "εξουσια," 352, "a state of control over something, freedom of choice, right."

[14] Leon J. Podles, *The Church Impotent: The Feminization of Christianity* (Dallas, TX: Spence, 1999), 3.

[15] R. Paul Stevens, *Liberating the Laity* (Downers Grove, IL: InterVarsity, 1985), 147.

CHAPTER 12

Helping the Weak, the Blessing of Giving, Bidding Farewell

In all things I have shown you that by working hard in this way we must help the weak and remember the words of the Lord Jesus, how he himself said, "It is more blessed to give than to receive."
(Acts 20:35)

And when he had said these things, he knelt down and prayed with them all. And there was much weeping on the part of all; they embraced Paul and kissed him, being sorrowful most of all because of the word he had spoken, that they would not see his face again. And they accompanied him to the ship.
(Acts 20:36–38)

We come now to Paul's final point and an essential part of the shepherding task—caring for those who are "weak." Not only was Paul not greedy for money, he was big-hearted and compassionate, eager to help the poor and needy.

Holding up his own example before the elders, he said,

You yourselves know that these hands ministered to my necessities and to those who were with me. In all things *I have shown you that by working hard in this way we must help the weak.* (Acts 20:34–35)

By his own impressive example, Paul set the tone for the church and its elders *to lovingly care for its weak and needy members.*

"I HAVE SHOWN YOU"

Paul concluded his message the same way he began it: pointing the elders to his own life example. The great truths of the gospel must be fleshed out in the lives of godly examples for others to observe and follow. We need people who live out the truth if the truth is to be believed by others. Paul was such a man. The public Paul was the same as the private Paul. There was no disconnect between what he preached and how he lived. He was a man of integrity and Christlike character. Some have called this "character leadership."

Here he says, "In all things I have shown you" (v. 35). John Wooden, a legendary basketball coach, is well-known for saying, "The most powerful leadership tool you have is your personal example."[1] There are certain things in life we cannot learn from books. In fact, we learn a great deal more than we realize by watching the examples set by those around us, like our parents, peers, and heroes. We copy other people far more than we like to admit. Paul's example left a permanent impression.

Lasting Memories

Let me illustrate. At this very moment, I can go back in my mind 60 years to when I became a born-again Christian. There is much I have forgotten from that time, and I cannot remember most of the sermons I heard. But I still vividly remember what it was like to go to a Bible-believing church for the first time, to meet people who really loved the Lord and his Word.

I can remember how the people were dressed, how they publicly prayed and sang, how they loved the Bible, how they drove me to church every Sunday morning and evening, how they invited me into their homes, and how they loved on me. I can see all of this in my mind clearly, even many decades later. The example of those believers' sincere devotion to Christ and his Word is burned into my memory for ever.

> "[Be] examples to the flock." 1 Peter 5:3

Paul understood the power of human example to influence people for good or for bad. While Timothy was in Ephesus seeking to correct an alarming situation, Paul urged him to "set the believers an example in speech, in conduct, in love, in faith, in purity" (1 Tim. 4:12). *Timothy was also to lead by example.*

The apostle Peter charged the elders to be "examples to the flock" (1 Peter 5:3). You may have a job that calls you "pastor," or a badge identifying you as "elder" or "deacon." But it is not your title that will influence people for God; it is your godly character and loving actions that will give you credibility and influence people for good.

Seizing Every Opportunity to Teach

Using every opportunity, Paul set forth[2] an example that would forever teach the Ephesian elders the value of hard work and the duty of compassionate care for those in need: *"In all things I have shown you that by working hard in this way we must help the weak"* (v. 35).

Hard Work

The Greek verb for "working hard" (κοπιάω [*kopiaō*]) is a strong word, stressing physical exertion to the point of weariness.[3] Christians are not to be idle or lazy loafers waiting for others to support them. Laziness is a moral issue and a terrible witness to the transforming power of the gospel before a skeptical, unbelieving world. Paul makes this point most forcefully to the new believers in Thessalonica:

> Now we command you, brothers, in the name of our Lord Jesus Christ, that you keep away from any brother who is walking in idleness and not in accord with the tradition that you received from us. For you yourselves know how you ought to imitate us, because *we were not idle when we were with you*, nor did we eat anyone's bread without paying for it, but with toil and labor we worked night and day, that we might not be a burden to any of you. It was not because we do not have that right, but *to give you in ourselves an example to imitate*. For even when we were with you, we would give you this command: If anyone is not willing to work, let him not eat. For we hear that some among you walk in idleness, not busy at work, but busybodies. Now such persons we command and encourage in the Lord Jesus Christ to do their work quietly and to earn their own living. (2 Thess. 3:6–12; also 1 Thess. 4:11–12; Eph. 6:5–8)

Creation Design: Paul's teachings follow God's original design for the human race. From the beginning, God made the man and woman to work. It was his good intention for them to work and to be creative and productive. Work is a blessing from God! But when sin entered the world, so did human laziness (especially spiritual laziness) and indiscipline, resulting in wasted lives, squandered talents, and human poverty.

Working Hard for Christ: For Spirit-indwelt believers, work takes on new meaning. In all our labor, we serve the Lord Christ himself, not just an employer. "Whatever you do, *work heartily, as for the Lord and not for men*, knowing that from the Lord you will receive the inheritance as your reward" (Col. 3:23–24). As an employee, you are to serve

> with a sincere heart, as you would Christ, not by the way of eye-service, as people-pleasers, but as bondservants of Christ, doing the will of God from the heart, rendering service with a good will as to the Lord and not to man. (Eph. 6:5–7)

Paul deliberately established himself as an example of hard work for the new believers to imitate. The clause "working hard in this way" included working at his trade of tentmaking, his pastoral duties, and his gospel proclamation. In all that he did, Paul was "serving the Lord" (v. 19) and providing for others an excellent role model of the Christian work ethic.

As role models for the Lord's people,
you are to set an example of hard work,
self-discipline, and self-sacrifice.

Setting an Example: As role models for the Lord's people, you are to set an example of hard work, self-discipline, and self-sacrifice. This is not meant to make work an idol of pride or to endorse workaholism, which is unhealthy spiritually and physically. All of life's responsibilities—family, work, church—need to be held in balance, and this is never easy to do. Each week my wife and I go over our calendars together, in order to take control of our schedules and the many demands placed upon us, to do our best to balance out life's busyness.

"Contribute to the needs of the saints." Romans 12:13

Must Help the Weak

Working hard to make money is not to be an end in itself. By earning money, we are able to share some of our monetary resources to "help the weak." Again, in word and deed Paul used every opportunity to communicate the value of sharing one's earnings with those in need.

This was a matter dear to Paul's heart because giving to those in need is an expression of Christian love. In the context of showing genuine Christian love to one another (Rom. 12:9–21), Paul exhorted the Christians in Rome to "contribute to the needs of the saints" (Rom. 12:13).

The Weak: In Acts 20:35, "the weak" are those who cannot secure basic physical and material necessities[4] due to age, sickness, disability, poverty, social status, or any other legitimate reason. Paul is not referring to spiritually weak Christians, but to those in the body who need financial, medical, or personal assistance.

The weak may be people who cannot work and meet their own needs, much less give anything in return for the help they receive. Some of these people would be widows. Addressing the situation with the church in Ephesus, Paul wrote Timothy, who was Paul's representative there, fourteen verses about the care of widows (1 Tim. 5:3–16; see also Acts 6:1–7). In those times, widows and orphans faced deplorable poverty; they were often ignored or exploited by unscrupulous people. It is these kinds of disadvantaged people that the elders must help by drawing from their own funds. As Paul wrote: "Let the thief no longer steal, but rather let him labor, doing honest work with his own hands, so that he may have something to share with anyone in need" (Eph. 4:28).

Must Help: Care for the poor was a matter of sincere concern for Paul. He knew very well the many Old Testament directives that God's people *must* care for the widow, the orphan, the foreigner, and the poor. This was not a suggestion; it was a divine command.

By using the word "must" (δεῖ [*dei*]), and by quoting the Lord Jesus, Paul made this a biblical and moral obligation especially for the elders. Part of the elders' job is to make sure the "weak" members of God's flock receive proper assistance: "we *must* help the weak."

When James, Peter, and John asked Paul to remember the many poor believers in the city of Jerusalem, Paul's response was that it was "the very thing I was eager to do" (Gal. 2:10). Paul demonstrated his eagerness by expending a great deal of effort organizing a financial offering from the Gentile churches for the poverty-stricken saints in Jerusalem. He even made the long journey with church representatives to deliver the contribution to the elders in Jerusalem.

> Part of the elders' job is to make sure the "weak" members of God's flock receive proper assistance: "we must help the weak."

Qualification: One of the biblical qualifications for an overseeing elder is that he be "a lover of good" (Titus 1:8), which, "according to the interpretation of the early Church, . . . relates to the unwearying activity of love."[5] One Greek lexicon defines the word here (φιλάγαθος [*philagathos*]) as "one who willingly and *with self-denial* does good, or is kind."[6]

An elder who is "a lover of good" does good deeds. He helps others through his kindness and love, especially those who are "weak" and require material assistance. He sets the example for the congregation of loving what is good.

THE BLESSING OF GIVING GENEROUSLY

To emphasize his instructions, Paul called on his colleagues to remember something Jesus said: "It is more blessed to give than to receive." This saying, in the form of a beatitude, is not found in any of the four Gospels. Rather it was one of Jesus's expressions passed down orally among the Christians. This theme of giving generously to others in need was part of Jesus's overall teaching on money, which included warnings about the corrupting power of greed and the problem of hoarding wealth.

Jesus's Financial Advice

Since Jesus is Lord, his words are authoritative and must be remembered and obeyed. *For the Christian there is no higher source of authority than the words of our Lord.* Paul's whole outlook on money and giving was derived directly from the teachings of Jesus Christ. For example, Jesus said:

> Fear not, little flock, for it is your Father's good pleasure to give you the kingdom. *Sell your possessions, and give [alms] to the needy.* Provide yourselves with moneybags that do not grow old, with *a treasure in the heavens* that does not fail, where no thief approaches and no moth destroys. For where your treasure is, there will your heart be also. (Luke 12:32–34; also see Luke 3:11; 6:38; 10:25–37; 12:13–31; 14:12–14; 16:13; 18:22)

Treasures in Heaven: Jesus provided his "little flock" with the wisest financial advice ever given: Invest your money (and time) in eternal treasures in heaven, not in earthly treasures, which are not secure or eternal.

Moreover, Jesus said that where one's treasure is, there one's true affections lie. So, where is the treasure that your heart is fixed upon?

> Invest your money (and time) in eternal treasures
> in heaven, not in earthly treasures, which
> are not secure or eternal.

Furthermore, Jesus declared that it is impossible to serve two masters—"God and money"—at the same time (Luke 16:13). He also said that we are not to be overly anxious about the material matters of life, but "instead, seek his kingdom, and these things will be added to you" (Luke 12:31; also Luke 18:29–30).

Jesus especially warned his followers against the sin of greed and perverse love for earthly possessions:

Take care, and be on your guard against all covetousness [greed], for one's life does not consist in the abundance of his possessions. (Luke 12:15; also Luke 11:39; 12:16–21)

The Virtue of Generosity: It is Jesus's instructions to give to those in need, and his warnings regarding the corrupting power of greed, that explain the extravagant display of generosity by the first Christians: "And they were selling their possessions and belongings and distributing the proceeds to all, as any had need" (Acts 2:45).[7]

In Paul's letter to Timothy and the church in Ephesus, he echoed the words of Jesus:

As for the rich in this present age, charge them not to be haughty, nor to set their hopes on the uncertainty of riches, but on God, who richly provides us with everything to enjoy. They are to do good, to be rich in good works, *to be generous and ready to share,* thus storing up treasure for themselves as a good foundation for the future, *so that they may take hold of that which is truly life.* (1 Tim. 6:17–19)

In many practical ways, the gospel should affect our use of money and possessions, our wallets, and our bank accounts. As John Bunyan reminds us, "The soul of true religion is the practical part."[8] Christ's teachings connect our faith with our finances. As leaders and teachers among the Lord's people you need to teach and practice Jesus's monetary principles of living. Paul did!

"God loves a cheerful giver." 2 Corinthians 9:7

The Giving Beatitude

Young children naturally think that it is more blessed to receive gifts than to give gifts. They love Christmastime because they receive lots of gifts. But as a person matures in Christ, he or she begins to experience the joy and personal satisfaction of giving to others. To see one's money lift up others in need and gladden their hearts is a joy to one's soul. It really is "more blessed to give than to receive."

God Loves a Cheerful Giver: Those who experience the blessedness of giving can be encouraged to know that "God loves a cheerful giver" (2 Cor. 9:7). He loves them! That is an incredible thought. God sees and approves of the cheerful giver. Cheerful giving comes from a heart full of the love of God and love for neighbor. Cheerful giving also comes from a heart full of the Holy Spirit. Miserliness or stinginess is an anti-Christian attitude and is a work of the flesh. It is a contradiction to God's "inexpressible gift" of Christ (2 Cor. 9:15).

If you want your church to be known for generosity and Christlike compassionate care, then *you need to set the example of the blessedness of giving*. As role models for God's people, be like Jesus—compassionate, big-hearted, generous, and self-sacrificial. As one writer aptly puts it, "We must replace covetousness with liberality."[9]

A TEARFUL SEPARATION

An article from a Christian magazine spoke of the lonely pastor atop the leadership pyramid of the church. This may be a reality in some top-down organizations, but it should not be the case in the household of God, among brothers and sisters in Christ.

The lonely leader at the top is a poor example of Christlike leadership, and certainly not Paul's style. Paul was not a Diotrephes type, "who [liked] to put himself first" at the apex of the leadership pyramid (3 John 9). Paul loved those around him "with the affection of Christ Jesus" (Phil. 1:8). He was not distant or impersonal. He was a leader and teacher *who developed close personal relationships with people.*[10]

Paul had developed a close fraternal bond with the Ephesian elders. They loved him, and he loved them. He was profoundly thankful for their willingness to sacrificially serve as shepherd elders of the church. They had labored side-by-side in the gospel. As a result, these elders would be forever inspired by Paul's single-minded devotion to Christ and his love for people. Their lives had been permanently changed by his life. Good leaders not only can teach and manage, but more importantly, *they inspire others to press forward for God. It is within the context of a close, working relationship with a mentor that some of the most effective and long-lasting discipleship takes place.*

At the conclusion of Paul's speech, Luke records this touching farewell scene:

> And when [Paul] had said these things, he knelt down and prayed with them all. And there was much weeping on the part of all; they embraced Paul and kissed him, being sorrowful most of all because of the word he had spoken, that they would not see his face again. And they accompanied him to the ship. (Acts 20:36–38)

Prayer

Paul and the elders "knelt down and prayed." Prayer was the only fitting conclusion to their final meeting. They knelt out of humility, dependence, and reverence before the throne of God. They were not kneeling before Paul, but before their Creator and Redeemer whom Paul had preached, and they had accepted as true.

The final scene is a moving one of weeping, kissing, and embracing: "And there was much weeping on the part of all; they embraced Paul and kissed him" (vv. 36–38). These were tears of love and sorrow. They were all beloved brothers in Christ.

Finally, the elders accompanied Paul to his ship. From there, he headed to Jerusalem, and they returned to Ephesus to continue their work of shepherding the church of God there.

PREPARING PASTORAL ELDERS FOR THE FUTURE

Acts 20 is a good example of the apostle passing his responsibilities of leading and teaching to those he had trained and prepared. There is probably no area in which local churches and their leaders fail more than in deliberately and systematically preparing the next generation of pastoral elders. Very few churches have a vision for training the future generation of leaders, or even educating and mentoring the present generation.

Failing to Train

After I spoke one evening at a church, a man asked if he could share his story with me. He hoped I would share it with other churches.

When this brother graduated from seminary, he returned home without a job. Shortly afterward, he was asked by a nearby church if he would fill in as an interim pastor until they found a permanent one. He spent a number of years temporarily filling in for churches that were looking for permanent pastors. But in all his years as interim pastor, he had not found one church that was seriously preparing its men for long-term church leadership. He never saw any concerted effort to teach men to study Scripture for themselves so they could know and understand Bible doctrine. Men in the churches were not being prepared to teach others, or to be involved in the pastoral leadership. There was no true New Testament eldership in any of these churches.

As a result, when the pastor left, there was an immediate and gaping void because no one else in the church was prepared to continue the teaching and pastoral ministry. The men of the church were completely clergy dependent. They did not think they were equipped to carry on the pastoral leadership of the church, nor had they been taught that this was something they should do. Indeed, they felt incapable and ill-prepared to do much of anything but find a replacement for the pastor. (To be fair, these churches had never seen an example of a biblical eldership, so it would be difficult for them to imagine pastoral leadership by a plurality of qualified, biblical elders.)

My friend saw this same situation in all his churches over his years as an interim pastor. He wanted me to tell people about his experience because it vividly demonstrates the widespread failure of churches to intentionally challenge and prepare its most qualified men for pastoral eldership.

> "What you have heard from me . . . entrust to faithful men who will be able to teach others also." 2 Timothy 2:2

Without training and effort there can be no biblical, pastoral eldership in a church. This is a tragedy because *a biblical eldership can provide a local church with long-term leadership stability and continuity of sound doctrine and practice.* It is also a serious disregard of Paul's charge to Timothy and to us today: "What you have heard from me in the presence of many witnesses entrust to faithful men who will be able to teach others also" (2 Tim. 2:2).

Pray, Plan, and Persevere, But Don't Give Up

If you feel overwhelmed and inadequate for the task of training future pastoral leaders for your church, don't let discouragement deter you. Most other people feel the same way. But there is a path forward.

Here are some practical resources to get started mentoring future shepherd leaders:

- Utilize the study guide to this book. You can find it free online at www.Acts20book.com. A teacher's guide is also provided and recommended for those who lead an Acts 20 study and discussion. This will ensure that you get the right answers in order to effectively help the students.

- For a more in-depth biblical study of eldership, read *Biblical Eldership: An Urgent Call to Restore Biblical Church Leadership* by Alexander Strauch. *The Study Guide to Biblical Eldership: Twelve Lessons for Mentoring Elders* is an invaluable resource for training future shepherd elders. It is designed to be used under the direction of a mentoring elder, but can also be used in a group setting. Thousands of churches worldwide have used this study guide with success.

  For the mentoring elder or group leader, there is a separate leader's guide titled *The Mentor's Guide to Biblical Eldership*. It includes background information, extensive answers to the study guide questions, and practical mentoring tips. For more information on these resources, go to www.LewisandRoth.com.

- In addition to your reading, another helpful resource is www. BiblicalEldership.com. Included on this website is The School of the Shepherds, an online training course for current and future elders. The curriculum consists of six courses each comprised of nine 15-minute videos. Furthermore, the website contains other materials for finding help for the various aspects of shepherding and teaching. This website is an excellent way to develop your present elders and train future elders.

- A final recommendation is Joseph H. Hellerman's book *Embracing Shared Ministry: Power and Status in the Early Church and Why It Matters Today*. This book is a must-read for all elders. Hellerman examines the biblical texts regarding church leadership against the backdrop of ancient Roman culture, providing valuable context for Paul's teachings. The book also contains study questions, making it a good group study resource for elder teams.

CONCLUSION

I end this book where we began: God has given us a special gift in Paul's farewell message to the Ephesian elders. There is really nothing else in the New Testament comparable to this passage. It is the only place in the New Testament in which Paul directly speaks to the church's elders, giving them their final marching orders. Bernard Aubert describes Paul's Miletus address as "a pastoral farewell"[11]—an accurate description.

Paul's instructions and pleas to the Ephesian elders are just as urgently needed today as they were that day on the shores of Miletus. History amply demonstrates that the truths of Paul's message cannot be overstated or repeated too often. The appalling, centuries-long failure to stop false teachers from invading churches can be traced directly back to ignorance of or disobedience to Paul's prophetic warnings to the Ephesian elders. Every new generation of church leaders needs to discover afresh Paul's instructions in Acts 20.

Any church elder who does not know the content of Paul's message is ill-equipped to lead and protect God's people. Acts 20 is the Holy Spirit's summons to you to come, hear, learn, and then shepherd God's church according to God's instructions. I challenge you to make it your goal to master the content of Paul's prophetic, apostolic message—study it, memorize it, think deeply upon it, discuss it, teach it, and live it. If you invest the time to prayerfully study and meditate on this God-given challenge to all Christ's undershepherds, you will find warnings and exhortations essential to the task, as well as fresh motivation and divine comfort.

Acts 20 is the Holy Spirit's summons to you
to come, hear, learn, and then shepherd God's
church according to God's instructions.

KEY POINTS TO REMEMBER

1. The shepherding task must include caring for those who are "weak" and needy.

2. By using the word "must" and by quoting the Lord Jesus, Paul set a biblical and moral obligation to ensure that the "weak" members of God's flock receive proper assistance.

3. Work is a blessing from God! But when sin entered the world, so did human laziness (especially spiritual laziness) and lack of discipline. This resulted in wasted lives, squandered talents, and human poverty.

4. It truly is more blessed to give financially to those in need than to receive.

5. A biblical eldership can provide a local church with long-term stability of leadership and continuity of sound doctrine and practice.

6. Without serious training and effort there can be no biblical, pastoral eldership in a church.

---

[1] Barry Demp, ed., "Powerful Leadership," The Quotable Coach, 2016, https://www.thequotablecoach.com/powerful-leadership/.

[2] BDAG, s.v., "ὑποδείγνυμι," 1037: "to give instruction or moral direction, show, give direction, prove, set forth."

[3] BDAG, s.v. "κοπιάω," 558: "to exert oneself physically, mentally, or spiritually, work hard, toil, strive, struggle."

[4] BDAG, s.v. "ἀσθενέω," 142: "to experience lack of material necessities, be in need."

[5] Walter Grundmann, "φιλάγαθος," in TDNT, 1 (1964):18.

[6] Hermann Cremer, *Biblico-Theological Lexicon of New Testament Greek*, trans. W. Urwick (Edinburgh: T&T Clark, 1895), s.v. "φιλάγαθος," 9.

[7] See Acts 2:44–45; 4:32–5:11; 6:1–7.

[8] John Bunyan, *The Pilgrim's Progress* (Abbotsford, WI: Life Sentence Publishing, 2014), 95.

[9] William J. Larkin, Jr., Acts, IVPNTC (Downers Grove, IL: InterVarsity, 1995), 299.

[10] See Alexander Strauch, *A Christian Leader's Guide to Leading with Love* (Littleton, CO: Lewis & Roth, 2006), 91–98. This is a chapter about how Paul expressed love and affection.

[11] Bernard Aubert, "The Shepherd-Flock Motif in the Miletus Discourse Against Its Historical Background," *Studies in Biblical Literature*, no. 124 (New York: Peter Lang Publishing, 2009), 109.

Name Index

Scripture Index

Subject Index

ACKNOWLEDGMENTS

Christian friends are a special gift from the good hand of God. I am an exceedingly blessed man to have many skilled friends who assisted me in the completion of this book.

I gladly acknowledge special friends who have followed me from the beginning of this project. I am indebted to Anne Swartley who donated many hours to reading, correcting, and editing this book. A great deal of gratitude is extended to Jay Brady, Operations Manager at Lewis & Roth Publishers, who helped me at every phase of the production of this work. Without the help of my gifted Administrative Assistant, Lisa Corbett, I would still be in the process of writing this book. Many thanks are also due to Allan Sholes for his final editorial work.

I have asked a number of scholars to evaluate the exegesis, arguments, and interpretations in this book. They have made significant contributions to the technical aspects of this work. Thanks to Dr. David MacLeod and Dr. Larry Dixon for their many suggestions and cautions.

I thank all those who helped by reading the manuscript and providing me with comments. You know who you are.

As always, my deepest appreciation goes to my loving wife Marilyn, my chief partner in life and in the work of the Lord.

ADDITIONAL RESOURCES

These resources from Alexander Strauch will help you and your church nuture the love described in 1 Corinthians 13. They are available through your favorite bookseller or through the publisher.

LewisandRoth.com

800.477.3239 (USA) | 719.494.1800 (International)

A Christian Leader's Guide to Leading with Love

Based on careful exposition of Scripture, Strauch presents the New Testament passages on love and applies them to leading people according to the "more excellent way" (1 Cor. 12:31). Whatever your leadership role is, you will be convicted, challenged and inspired to lead in the way of Christlike love.

A study guide is also available, making this a valuable tool for group study.

"This message is urgently needed by all of us. You may have talents and spiritual gifts, but without the love that his book talks about, you don't really have much at all."
— George Verwer, Founder, Operation Mobilization

Love or Die: Christ's Wake-up Call to the Church

In his challenging exposition of Revelation 2:2–6, Strauch examines this alarming rebuke of Jesus Christ to his church. *Love or Die* reminds us that love can grow cold while outward religious performance appears acceptable—even praiseworthy.

A five-lesson study guide is included in the book.

"I can think of few books I've read recently that have had so immediate an impact on me and have given me so much to think about. I trust, that with God's help, the implications of this book will be with me always." — Tim Challies, challies.com

Lewis & Roth Publishers
800.477.3239 • www.lewisandroth.com

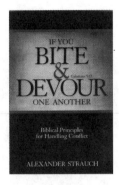

If You Bite & Devour One Another: Biblical Principles for Handling Conflict

Conflict in churches is a pervasive problem we know all too well. In *If You Bite & Devour One Another*, Strauch examines the biblical passages on conflict and discusses key scriptural principles for handling various kinds of conflicts among Christians. The book emphasizes Spirit-controlled attitudes and behaviors through solid exposition and true-to-life stories of Christians handling conflicts in a Christ-honoring way.

A free study guide is also available for download at www.lewisandroth.com/free-downloads/.

"This book is urgently needed in the body of Christ.... I have put *Bite & Devour* into the top ten books that we are getting out across the world. It's a must read."
— George Verwer, Founder, Operation Mobilization

Agape Leadership: Lessons in Spiritual Leadership from the Life of R. C. Chapman

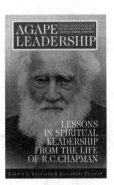

Agape Leadership promises to be one of the most spiritually inspiring books you've read. R. C. Chapman (1803–1902) provides an extraordinary example of Christlike, loving leadership. Charles Spurgeon, who knew Chapman, referred to him as "the saintliest man I ever knew."

Chapman became legendary in his own time for his gracious ways, his patience, his ability to reconcile people in conflict, his absolute fidelity to Scripture, and his loving pastoral care. By the end of his life, Chapman was know worldwide for his love, wisdom and compassion. In *Agape Leadership*, you will see godly, pastoral leadership in action through biographical snapshots from Chapman's life.

"This book . . . should be read by everyone who calls on Christ as Lord. In so doing, you will be challenged to arrange your life in such a way that you are finding Christ to be your greatest and first love." — Terry Delaney, Christian Book Notes

Lewis & Roth Publishers
800.477.3239 • www.lewisandroth.com

Biblical Eldership
by Alexander Strauch

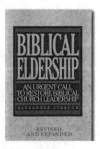

With more than 200,000 copies in print and translated into more than 30 languages, *Biblical Eldership* is a comprehensive look at the role and function of elders, bringing all the advantages of shared leadership into focus. *Biblical Eldership* explores the essential work of elders, their qualifications, their relationships with each other, and each of the biblical passages related to eldership. Written for those seeking a clear understanding of the mandate for biblical eldership, this book defines it accurately, practically and according the Scripture.

"Best exegetical overview of eldership around today."
— Kevin DeYoung, Pastor,
University Reformed Church

"For churches to thrive they need to be led by men who follow the Scriptures. Strauch wonderfully instructs us on the character qualifications needed to serve as elders and the responsibilities incumbent on elders. This book is a valuable resource for courses on pastoral ministry and is highly recommended for every church."
— Thomas R. Schreiner, Associate Dean,
The Southern Baptist Theological Seminary

"[This] excellent book . . . is the definitive work on the subject. . . . The book deserves wide distribution and I plan to do whatever I can to insure this."
— William MacDonald, Author,
Believer's Bible Commentary

Additional resources for training and equipping elders:

- *Biblical Eldership Study Guide*
- *Biblical Eldership Mentor's Guide*
- *Biblical Eldership Booklet*
- *Biblical Eldership Discussion Guide*

Lewis & Roth Publishers
800.477.3239 • www.lewisandroth.com